Closer to God

Closer to God

Don't keep fighting the darkness; turn on the Light…
Don't keep pushing out evil; let in the Good…

EDUARDO VILLEGAS

Library of Congress Control Number:		2015902295
ISBN:	Hardcover	978-1-5065-0021-8
	Softcover	978-1-5065-0020-1
	eBook	978-1-5065-0019-5

Print information available on the last page.

Rev. date: 23/02/2015

To order additional copies of this book, please contact:
Palibrio
1663 Liberty Drive
Suite 200
Bloomington, IN 47403
Toll Free from the U.S.A 877.407.5847
Toll Free from Mexico 01.800.288.2243
Toll Free from Spain 900.866.949
From other International locations +1.812.671.9757
Fax: 01.812.355.1576
orders@palibrio.com
706074

CONTENTS

INTRODUCTION

"The heavens declare the glory of God; And the firmament shows His handiwork."

Psalm 19:1

Every night before going to sleep, I like to contemplate the sky from the back yard of my house. I like to go to bed with that sensation of God's greatness, of the transcendence of life, and not with my mind full of my little worries. When I think about the distances that separate us from the planets, from the stars and other galaxies, I can do nothing less than be amazed at God's work. How beautiful that what we see today in the sky is the same that David saw three thousand years ago! And that we can conclude with him that "the heavens declare," that is, they speak of His glory. They reflect His greatness and make us imagine His splendor, His magnificence. The question is simple: if this is what creation is like, what will the Creator be like? And the verse later adds that the "firmament announces," meaning it proclaims, declares the work, the creation of His hands. God's work has His fingerprint clearly impressed upon it; one doesn't need to be a genius to see that God is behind every detail of His infinite creation.

Today, while you begin a new day or go running from one activity to another, from one appointment to the next, in the middle of your homework or in traffic, remember that there is a God so powerful that He created the heavens and the earth so you would think about Him, and that He loves you so much that he gave up His beloved son to give you abundant life; wellbeing, freedom, and fullness. Don't let little daily traps distract you. Don't let yourself be overwhelmed by stress and worry. Keep your mind focused on His greatness, and you will see that God is revealing Himself to you, in your spouse, in your children, in your table and in your work, or in a piece of music; in the rain, in the breeze, in a smile or a hug; in the little miracles that some call coincidences, and yes, even in your mirror. Don't ignore Him. Despite the noise and the bedlam, pay attention, because the heavens declare Him and the firmament announces Him. Don't let the small things distract you from what is relevant, and don't let the important hide behind the banal.

Today, more than ever, it is urgent and necessary that we learn to see inside, to observe more deeply, to realize the huge and beautiful details that we have in front of us, but that our unaware and distracted (perhaps I should say untrained) mind has become used to ignoring.

> *"For since the creation of the world His invisible attributes are clearly seen, being understood by the things that are made, even His eternal power and Godhead, so that they are without excuse,"*
> Romans 1:20

The Bible is a book inspired by the Holy Spirit, and it contains the Word that is the Word: Christ. It is a completely supernatural and inexhaustible book that contains the power to change our lives, much more than the sum of all the good books that have ever been written. Personally, I have learned that when a Bible verse, or a portion of it, penetrates and touches the most intimate fibers of my inner being, my mind keeps meditating on that Word without any effort for hours and sometimes days. During this process, I can understand how that Word touches deep aspects of my life and transforms my way of thinking, living, behaving and seeing the world. It is exciting to see the renewing and healing effect of the Word inside us; to be loosed by the strength of the Holy Spirit and feel how we are restored, while the strongholds in our mind crumble, making us more centered on God and giving us a broader perspective--less critical and more compassionate, less rigid and more happy, flexible, complete, and wise, with a deep sense of belonging and a life mission. In that process I discover more of God's will for me, many times understanding the reasons why I go through certain circumstances and challenges, and so gaining a little more light on the whole picture that God has prepared for me. In this way, I can open my mind and start to live **Closer to God**.

Closer to God contains seventy-five daily biblical reflections that will help you to draw near and stay connected to the only Source of life and good. These meditations on His Word will help you stay focused on what is Higher in the middle of your daily living.

Dedicated to everyone who is spiritually hungry, and as such,

- does not find answers or satisfaction in religions,
- understands that he cannot get to Heaven by his own discernment, but that it requires the help of Him who descended from Heaven (John 3:13)
- and wants to know the Father more …

With profound thanks:

- To the Holy Spirit, who has done everything
- To my family, who inspires everything in me
- To my readers, the reason for everything

PROLOGUE

At one opportunity, Jesus said, *"No one has ascended to heaven but He who came down from heaven, that is, the Son of Man <u>who is in heaven</u>."*[1] Jesus calls Himself the Son of Man to confirm that, although he was born without sin, he became completely human. For that reason, when He presents himself to doubting Thomas, he says, "Behold My hands and My feet, that it is I Myself. Handle Me and see, for a spirit does not have flesh and bones as you see I have."[2] However, although he was talking to His disciples in the land of Israel, He tells them (in present tense) that He "is in heaven." So, was He in heaven or on Earth?

At another moment, the Master told Peter that everything that he bound on Earth would be bound in heaven, and everything loosed on Earth would be loosed in heaven.[3] Throughout the whole Bible, the relationship between the invisible, spiritual world and the natural, visible world is clear. Although our eyes can't perceive it, every action, every decision, and everything that happens on earth causes an impact, a consequence, a reaction, in the spiritual realm. Paul asserts, "we walk by faith, not by sight,"[4] "while we do not look at the things which are seen, but at the things which are not seen. For the things which are seen are temporary,

---

1   John 3:13
2   Luke 24:39
3   Matthew 16:19
4   2 Corinthians 5:7

but the things which are not seen are eternal."[5] The invisible world is more real than the one that we can perceive, but unfortunately, the latter takes up the majority (if not all) of our attention.

But Jesus, having His spiritual eyes completely open, lived simultaneously in both worlds, although he certainly gave priority to the spiritual. I believe that was one of His keys to being able to accomplish all His work in only thirty-three years. For this reason also, when He taught His disciples to pray, part of the prayer says "Your Kingdom come" and also "Your will be done on earth as it is in heaven,"[6] so there is a kingdom in the spiritual that we should ask to come to earth, or to the earthly, to our lives, to our day by day. We cannot keep living disconnected from God, focused only on what we see. It's like living by the sea and staying on the surface, and never diving in.

It is important that we learn to live in both kingdoms at the same time. That we maintain an active spiritual perspective during our busy schedule, so we see every circumstance within its real dimension. But this doesn't mean we create our own kingdom through concentration or meditation, producing our own mental "garden" where we take refuge. You should know that just like on earth, good and evil exist in the spiritual world. You shouldn't venture into it without Jesus. Neither does it mean staying positive by repeating memorized optimistic formulas. This is about being attentive to the Kingdom of God, to the Heavens, while we walk, daily, on this earth. That is the objective of this work.

---

5   2 Corinthians 4:18

6   Matthew 6:10

A daily devotional that is accessible to you so that in the middle of the bustle, stress, and apparent instability we live in, you can also be "Closer to God."

Father, forgive me when I invent who You are instead of spending time with you to know You…

To know more of You, I need to be <u>closer to You.</u>

Transform me by the renewing of my mind!
Romans 12:2

A NOTE:

This book in no way attempts to substitute the daily Bible reading that is the Word of God and the daily Bread of every true believer. This work is only one way, among many others, to encourage you to begin a relationship with God's Holy Spirit, so that you can live "Closer to God."

All biblical references are quoted from the New King James Version, unless otherwise noted.

All emphases and underlined phrases in these biblical quotes were added by the author.

SUGGESTIONS FOR READING THIS BOOK:

- *Try to only read the theme of the day. It is best not to read ahead.*
- *Choose an accessible place for this book, perhaps your nightstand, a seat in your car or in your bag or briefcase.*
- *Declare the title of the daily theme, at the top of the page, out loud.*
- *Review your reading as many times as possible, but at least in the morning and again at the end of the day, ideally before going to bed. Remember that you only need a minute each time.*
- *Take a few moments to order your thoughts around the day's reading. That will help your thoughts to remain on the meditated idea. If possible, write your reflections about that day and three key words that stick out to you in a notebook.*

- *Also, it's a good idea to share your reading with a loved one or friend.*
- *If a theme particularly "touches" you, don't hesitate to keep reading that same page for the next day or more. As long as you feel God speaking to you through a verse, keep reading it, and go on to the next only when you feel that you have "squeezed" everything out of the former*

Let's begin…

Day 1: Today I lift up my soul to You, Lord

"To You, O Lord, I lift up my soul."

Psalm 25:1

When God "formed man from the dust of the ground, and breathed into his nostrils the breath of life," (Genesis 2:7a), Adam became a "living being" (1 Cor. 15:45a). The soul (from the Greek *psyche*) is what connects the body with the spirit in us, and is the place where our thoughts, feelings and emotions dwell, whether they are positive or negative, conscious or unconscious. It guides our behavior, and it is in the soul where we open up our greatest battles, because we decide in our soul if we live for the Spirit or for our flesh (ego). David, the Psalmist, was a man full of dreams and plans, challenges and passions, and lived in the midst of great threats and difficulties, just like you and me, but he was always successful because he knew a great secret: every day he "lifted up his soul to God."

Every day we act according to our soul: We react with a smile, a disparaging look or a malicious rumor, depending on the soul's condition. We make decisions according to the paradigms etched in it, and we cannot see dreams bigger than what fits in it. Even facing the same circumstance we can go forward with confidence or flee in terror, depending on the faith growing within the soul. The soul contains our fears and our potential, our wounds together with our scars, our dependence together with our liberty, our mistakes together with their restoration. We decide whether to focus our soul on the dust from which we were formed or on the Spirit that gave us life. Take a minute now, please. Bend over to the floor and pick up your shame and sadness, your fears and anxieties, the betrayals and that old dependence that makes you want to control everything, and lift them up to God. You will see how, in lifting them up, they dissolve like mist. Bend over and symbolically pick up the pieces of every one of your dreams, stick them together with the tears that each one still contains, and lift them up to the One who put them in your heart. You will realize that they are indeed possible, only in you, only through you... Lift up your arms, opening up your soul, and submit it to the Father, without disguises, without pretensions, naked. Undress your precious vulnerability and you will see how He makes you strong. Every day, when you open your eyes, lift your soul up to God; in every pause, every time that you can, lift up your soul and put it in the hands of the One who created you and gave Himself up so that you would be free.

> *"Cause me to know the way in which I should walk, For I lift up my soul to You."*
>
> Psalm 143:8b

Prayer: Holy Father: I recognize my vulnerability. I present myself before You without disguises, just as You created me. I lift up my soul to accept Your inspiration, Your dreams and Your guidance. Today I focus on You and I receive Your love. Thank you, Abba.

Day 2: Today I remember that You love me

"And the Holy Spirit descended in bodily form like a dove upon Him, and a voice came from heaven which said, 'You are My beloved Son; in You I am well pleased.'"

Luke 3:22

Jesus was being baptized when the Father declared these powerful words, reminding Him who He is. This is why He begins by saying, "You are." He doesn't say, "You have," nor does He say, "You do." What's more, He doesn't even call Him by the title of Messiah or Redeemer, because the Father was not saying who Jesus is to the world, what He should achieve or even how big His mission is. Abba (Daddy) is declaring who Jesus is for Him: "My Son." You are mine. You are my Son, and on top of that, "You are loved." And He adds, "in You I am well pleased." The translation of the original Greek for the words "well pleased" is "a delight, something that causes happiness, satisfaction, something that pleases." The love of the Father for the Son was exactly the same before and after Jesus's sacrifice on the Cross. This infinite love was not conditional to the circumstances; rather, it on top of it all. I believe that it can be easier to understand this love for those of us who have children. Sometimes I silently watch one of my children while they study, play, or even sleep, and the "well pleased" feeling simply overflows from my being.

It was not a coincidence that the Father chose this moment to remind Jesus of His identity. From there, He would go directly to the desert, to confront Satan for forty days while He fasted from food and drink. Where would the attacks come from? From His identity, like always (we should remember that the Devil is not creative). This is why he tempts Him, saying, "if you are the Son of God," trying to define how Jesus should act. But the Father encourages Him at the exact moment in which His Ministry began. What a good Father we have in Heaven! It was one thing to live with His parents as a carpenter, and quite another to defeat the evil one and death. This world would never forgive Him. How could he divest Himself of all His royalty and remain absolutely humble, even to the agony of the worst of deaths? Only by knowing who He is with certainty and having an infinite love for you and me. Now then, if Jesus Christ needed to hear these words form the Father to remain centered on His mission, don't you think you and I do as well? I get tears in my eyes to even imagine that my father could say those words but God does, not because of anything that I have achieved, not for my good behavior, but only for who I am to Him: His beloved child, in whom He is well pleased, just like you…

"We love Him because He first loved us."

1 John 4:19

Prayer: Thank You for Your love, Papa. It's incredible that You, being the Highest and the Divine have the humility to love me so much. Today, I receive Your love. Today I believe and confess that I am Your beloved child, in whom You are well pleased.

Day 3: Today I know that I love You, too

"And the Holy Spirit descended in bodily form like a dove upon Him, and a voice came from heaven which said, 'You are My beloved Son; in You I am well pleased."

Luke 3:22

Paul asserts that we are fellow heirs with Christ (Ephesians 3:6), which means that Jesus shares the Father's inheritance with us. But for that, you must understand who you are, not according to your behavior, but according to the God's Grace. It's urgent that you understand that God's love is not something that you earn with your morals or good performance; instead, it is a precious gift that He gave you from before the foundation of the world (Ephesians 1:4) and demonstrated two thousand years ago. Did you start loving your baby when he began to talk or to walk? Of course not! You loved him from when he was inside your wife's belly. God is a Father as well. He gave Jesus up, on a cross, twenty centuries before you were born, just because of love for you and me, so we would not suffer under the yoke of slavery. Why do you pay for an expensive medication when your child is sick? Because you value his health more than your money. Why would the Father send His beloved Son to die for us? Because He valued us that much, and there was no other option. He did not entertain the idea of leaving us in darkness and chose to sacrifice, so receive it: God loves you. Let Him reveal Himself to you. That is the truth, which is why you can say to Him, "I am Your beloved child, in whom You are well pleased."

So now, who belongs to whom: the Father to the Son, or vice versa? The so-called Lord's Prayer begins by declaring, "Our Father," so He also belongs to us. I speak of "my" children, but they speak of "their" daddy. Isn't it beautiful? Although parents loved their children first, the children, upon meeting their parents and growing together, begin to love the parents as well. With time, they move from "I love you because I need you," to "I need you because I love you." In the same way, we can invert this prayer, change the focus from us to Him, and tell Him, "You are my beloved Father, in whom I am well pleased," because He is also yours. You are the owner of a fraction of God, but a fraction of Him is infinite. You urgently need to spend time with God so you will be convinced of who you are, and not shaken by the labels of "if you were…" But for that, you need a relationship with Him, not a religion. It has to be real; you can't pretend. Love him with all your mind and heart, because religion doesn't make you a son but a slave. But His Grace says,

> *"Then you will call upon Me and go and pray to Me, and I will listen to you. And you will seek Me and find Me, when you search for Me with all your heart."*
>
> Jeremiah 29:12-13

Prayer: I love You, Father. Today I pray to You and I seek you with a sincere heart. You are my beloved Father, in whom I am well pleased. Thank you for being my Papa.

Day 4: Today I love others as You love me

"And the Holy Spirit descended in bodily form like a dove upon Him, and a voice came from heaven which said, 'You are My beloved Son; in You I am well pleased."

Luke 3:22

If Jesus, God's Son, full of Grace and Power, needed Words of validation from the Father, and if you and I still crave them (although we try to disguise our vulnerability), don't you think that your children need to hear them as well? Don't doubt in the least that the Devil will try to damage their identities also: "If you really were…" He will try to put labels on them that limit and degrade them so they focus more on their defects and ignore their own virtues, wanting to fill a mold with the world's stereotype, to deserve approval. Many people will try to label them so God's power in them lies dormant, and if they don't know who they really are, any label will confuse and distract them. That is why it is so important and urgent that they know they are loved, by you. Without being aware of it, their souls will falter without your words of validation, confirmation, and blessing. It is not optional. They need it. We have the responsibility of teaching them who they really are.

I invite you to bless each one of your children in the same style as the Father. At any moment of the day, and without any reason (not because they got good grades or scored a goal), and whether they are three years old or thirty, put your hands on his/her shoulders, look him/her firmly in the eyes and say, "You are my beloved son (or daughter), in whom I am well pleased and I delight. You make my life happier. I am so happy to be your dad (or mom) and to have you every day. I thank God every day for sending you to my family, for the privilege of having you as my child." We all need the validation of a father or other paternal figure. My children hear it daily because it is imperative that they know it, so that the world will not make them stumble with "if you were..." Your children need to understand that you love them with all your being, not because they achieve, but because they are; that your gigantic love is not conditional to their behavior, their morals, or their performance. Don't use the recognition to manipulate them at the cost of their self-esteem. Motivate them every day but don't damage their self-worth. Inspire them, but not through comparison. Validate them; don't damage them. This is more necessary than their clothes or a good education.

> *"Behold, children are a heritage from the Lord, The fruit of the womb is a reward."*
>
> Psalm 127:3

Prayer: Thank you, Lord, for teaching me to bless others. I want to be a good father to my children, imitating You. I bless my descendants. For each of my children and any other young person who is under my care. Today I find pleasure in them just like You do in me.

Day 5: There is nothing I can do: He loves me.

"Then you will call upon Me and go and pray to Me, and I will listen to you. And you will seek Me and find Me, when you search for Me with all your heart."

Jeremiah 29:12-13

God is not as interested in our good actions as He is in molding our hearts (Deuteronomy 4:29). Not as interested in our morals as He is in having His law written on our souls (Deuteronomy 6:6). He isn't seeking rituals but our friendship. He doesn't want repetitions or many words (Matthew 6:7); rather, He wants us to listen at His feet (Luke 10:38), spending time with us. He wants an intimate relationship with you through His Holy Spirit, not an external religion built on traditions and festivals. He doesn't demand that we change our behavior to come closer to Him. Instead, He wants us to come close first, to be able to transform us. God wants you to know that He is real and He is there, next to you, alive, powerful. He is not in objects, relics or disciplines: "Why do you seek the living among the dead?" (Luke 24:5b)

There is absolutely nothing that you can do to make God love you more. He already does, with His whole, powerful heart. You cannot, and you don't have to, get Him to accept you. He already did through the blood of Jesus Christ, which is why He said, "… the one who comes to Me I will by no means cast out." (John 6:37) In fact, there is nothing you can do to make Him reject you, because God loves you exactly as you are now, no matter your circumstances, your mistakes or even if you have rejected Him (23:34). No father expects his baby to behave appropriately to begin loving him, but he seeks his attention at all cost, and does everything possible to get a smile, a look, or a babbled "Dada" that only he understands. Your love was already there even before your children were born. Why do you think our Father is any different? He created you, He delights in who you are, in how you are. He knows your weaknesses, but He is also aware of your potential. He understands your whole past, but he has already projected a different and extraordinary future for you, next to Him. Stop trying to deserve His love; it isn't possible, because it's about His Grace. Get rid of all religion, the preconceptions and paradigms. What God wants is your attention, your heart, your trust; in a nutshell: your friendship. And that only happens spending time together, alone, in intimacy, prayer, and communion… Set apart time every day to shut yourself away with Papa,

> *"But you, when you go pray, go into your room, and when you have shut your door, pray to your Father who is in the secret place; and your Father who sees in secret will reward you openly."*
>
> Matthew 6:6

Prayer: Holy Spirit, today I renounce trying to deserve Your love and I receive the Grace of your precious blood on the Cross. I don't need more proof of Your love, and I don't need to prove anything to You. You love me. Thank you for being the way you are, Lord.

Day 6: God is mine

"Thus says the Lord, your Redeemer, the Holy One of Israel: 'I am the Lord your God, who teaches you to profit, who leads you by the way you should go.'"

Isaiah 48:17

The Creator shows us two facets of who He is: Our Redeemer, who paid the price caused by all our debts and all the mistakes of our past and freed us from being slaves, according to the Law, and who is also our God. Not only do we belong to Him, He belongs to us, like parents belong to our children. If you have more than one child, you know that the love of parents isn't diluted among brothers and sisters. When your second child was born, you didn't cut out a portion of love for the first; rather, a new, complete, unique love arose. It's the same way with God. He loves every one of His children the same, because He is love, but that love is for everyone, including you. God loves us as a people, clearly, but He also loves us individually, you and me. That's why I say God is yours. He is your God.

But if that doesn't seem like much to you, that God of yours, that has also already redeemed you is the one: "who teaches you to profit... who leads you by the way you should go." There is a lot that we need to learn, but not just to complete a duty. Rather, we do it because it is profitable, it is very useful, it is practical and it is applicable to each of our daily lives. The reason that God wants us to know His Word is so we can take advantage of it, so we know His will and His secrets, because it shows us how to live under the principles of Heaven on earth. It is not a group of religious commandments or a martyr's penitence, nor is it to make you feel like a sinner, because He redeemed you and made you free. It's about knowing His will. That's why God tells you: "Call to Me, and I will answer you, and show you great and mighty things, which you do not know." (Jeremiah 33:3) The Word "I will teach you to profit," does good for you, nurtures you, and prospers you. You have the benefit of knowing it, it brings you profit and blessings to learn it and treasure it, and that teaching also "leads you by the way you should go." That is why you feel good after studying it, after seeking His Presence, because your spirit has been fed and your mind renewed. Don't doubt it; you have a Good Father in Heaven, who is yours, who redeemed you, who invests His time in you and makes sure you prosper, that "teaches you to profit" and guides you in the way you should go. Thank you, Jesus!

> *"I will instruct you and teach you in the way you should go; I will guide you with My eye."*
>
> Psalm 32:8

Prayer: Thank you, Jesus, for being mine. You are my Lord, my God, my Father. Although I can't touch you or see you now, I know that a part of your powerful heart is mine. You have written my name there.

Day 7: Only He will satisfy your soul

"For He satisfies the longing soul, and fills the hungry soul with goodness."

Psalm 107:9

Your soul is your psyche; all those things psychologists study, like your thoughts, your emotions and feelings, and your will. It's the place where we are happy or depressed, in love or lonely. Where dreams and ambitions live together with our fears and frustrations, and where music pours out its echo. It is also the connection between the spirit (our divine part where we can unite with God) and our physical body; where we dwell and move. The three are interconnected, the three are important, and it is a grave error to want to develop one to the detriment of the other. It is more pleasant to pray when we are healthy than when we are sick, and we have more energy to exercise when we are inspired. The same Greek word is translated as both air and spirit: Pneuma (that's where we get the word pneumatic). When we try to steer a car with empty tires, the vehicle drives more slowly, unstable, and, if we insist on driving it that way, it will be damaged. The same thing happens with human beings. Life without the Spirit is empty, slow, and very damaging.

Throughout the whole Bible we can see that "man shall not live by bread alone" (because we are much more than a body) "but by every word that proceeds from the mouth of God." (Matthew 4:4) The breath of God, The Word, His Word, is what gives true life. The spirit needs to adore and exalt God daily, and the soul needs to be nourished with thoughts of peace, abundance and health through the power of the Holy Spirit.

Don't keep letting your soul take off wherever it wants to go; you should nurture it, strengthen it, and yes, even discipline it, with the Word of God. This Psalm is talking about those who rebel against God, and continue saying that "their soul abhorred all manner of food, and they drew near to the gates of death" (verse 18). Why did it not say their body? The soul doesn't eat meat or vegetables. Clearly, it is saying that what brought them close to death was the lack of the Word for their souls, the consequence of rejecting God. Do you know what they did then? They "... cried out to the Lord in their trouble, and He saved them out of their distresses" (verse 19). Only when their pride and rebellion broke were they able to cry out to God and recognize their hunger for Him. Do you know what the Lord gave them? It wasn't manna or quail meat, but His Word.

> *"He sent His word and healed them, and delivered them from their destructions."*
>
> Psalm 107:20

Prayer: Lord, today I recognize my spiritual hunger. Today I understand that physical foods satisfy my body but not my spirit. I need Your Word. I don't want to be spiritually starved. Light up my spirit with Your Spirit. Come to me, Jesus. Thank you for Your imminent Presence.

Day 8: Only He is the source

"Abide in Me, and I in you. As the branch cannot bear fruit of itself, unless it abides in the vine, neither can you, unless you abide in Me."

John 15:4

Jesus uses clear images from our visible world so that we can compare and understand what happens in the invisible world: He is the vine, the trunk; we are His branches. The trunk doesn't sprout from the branches; rather, the branches sprout from the trunk. Without the trunk, there are no branches. The branches depend on the trunk and cannot live without it. Only the branch that remains connected to the trunk stays alive, blooms, and gives fruit. Sometimes we cut a small branch with a flower and put it in a vase with water, with the hope that it stays beautiful, but although it absorbs precious liquid, it will not bear fruit but will instead dry out because of the absence of the trunk. No matter how much you try to substitute for it, after a while, it will die; and although it appeared healthy on the outside, it will perish, because the dryness begins from the inside.

Many people live separated from God (the trunk), but even so, appear well nourished. They produce more or less radiant flowers, but they don't bear real fruit. The little water absorbed by the branches without the trunk seems to nourish them, but it isn't enough, and like cut flowers (even when put in a vase full of water), they begin to dry out, on the inside first. Because of that, they desperately seek other sources, like money or their own glory, or power or fame, with the childish illusion that they will never shrivel, that they will never pass away. They collect a multitude of brilliant objects and plastic flowers. Instead of bees and butterflies they get flies, and they flee from the wind, rain and sun. They submit themselves to licentiousness, squeezing out a little sap, forgetting that it only comes from the trunk. Parties, drugs, alcohol, pills to sleep, pills to wake up, pure artificial sap, like someone who puts drops in their eyes and pretends they have been crying. Separation from the trunk gives the branch the illusion of independence, until it realizes that the wind that rocked and shook it while it was attached now pulls it away, without direction… Nothing can substitute for the trunk. No one can stay separated from Him. Without God, life is only an illusion. We can never be separated from Him. Don't fall in the trap. The only possible way to save the branch is by inserting it back into the trunk. Put yourself in Jesus Christ, in no one else…

> *"I am the vine, you are the branches. He who abides in Me, and I in him, bears much fruit; for without Me you can do nothing."*
>   John 15:5

Prayer: Holy Spirit, You are the source of all good. There is nothing good for me apart from You. Come, Jesus, and fill me with the spiritual sap of Your Word. Open my eyes and ears to perceive more of Your light. Thank You!

Day 9: I have His peace

"Peace I leave with you, My peace I give to you; not as the world gives to I give to you. Let not your heart be troubled, neither let it be afraid."

John 14:27

Jesus establishes two different forms of peace. One comes from the world and the other from Him. It is His ("my peace"), and only He can share it with us ("I give to you"). The system of the world, as Jesus calls it (Paul calls it "this century" or the "current way of things"), refers to the way that humanity operates outside the will of God, trying to guide themselves but causing much more suffering because of their ignorance and rebellion, trying the same old ideologies with a different name in every generation, hoping to reach an order that satisfies everyone, but dismally failing time and again, for millennia. John defines the fruit of this world without God: "For all that is in the world--the lust of the flesh, the lust of the eyes, and the pride of life--is not of the Father but is of the world" (1 John 2:16).

The problem is that the desires of the flesh, of the eyes and of the vanity that we have inside us are insatiable, so the peace that this world gives is temporary, illusive, volatile, subject to circumstances, to our ego, and also to our deepest fears. On top of this, you are the one who should follow it at all cost and reach it, and then fight to stay there, and ultimately, it will be the world who judges if you achieved it or not, defining who you are. The peace of Jesus, on the other hand, cannot be obtained if He doesn't give it. You can't buy it or steal it, earn it or deserve it. You have to want it and He has to give it to you, but, since it doesn't depend on you, once you receive it, it keeps flowing every minute of every hour of every day so that you "let not your heart be troubled, neither let it be afraid." Can you imagine living without fear, in His peace, full of confidence in God and yourself because He dwells in you? How would your life change if you could let up on a little of the pressure to reach the results that others expect? For that, you must first choose what type of peace you want, and then act. You can choose the world, fight with all your might in your own way, and you will only be successful if you reach what the world values and recognizes. You can also choose Jesus, fight with His might and in His way, and you will be successful if you reach what Jesus values. You decide. The second option certainly requires more faith, because you must defeat the world, but it is eternal. And it won't depend on your success or your cunning, but in how much you believe in Him…

> *"Who is he who overcomes the world, but he who believes that Jesus is the Son of God?"*
>
> 1 John 5:5

Prayer: Lord Jesus, at this moment I put my unstable peace, depending on the world and my circumstances, at Your feet. I accept the gift of Your peace. I renounce control because only You are God. I renounce living under the world's standards because I do not belong to it, but to You. Thank you for Your peace, Lord.

Day 10: Today I rest in God

"My soul, wait silently for God alone, For my expectation is from Him."

Psalm 62:5

David speaks to his own soul (feelings, thoughts and will) and instructs it (ordering himself) to just wait (have peace, trust, rest) in God. The king adored the Lord while he trained his own attitude and was trained in the Truth. Whether he found himself in the middle of difficulty or success, surrounded by death threats or the deep admiration of all his people, in the cold hardness of a cave (fleeing Saul) or in the abundant richness of his palace, this incredible man didn't rest in his brave, powerful, and loyal warriors, or in his warehouses full of gold ingots, or in his many qualities, virtues, and wisdom (1 Samuel 16:18). No, David understood that his life, just like yours and mine, is in the hands of the one God, and we can only rest in Him, that He is the only source of our hope. In fact, that He, the author of faith (Hebrews 12:2), is the owner of it. This is why Paul says that we have been "bought with a price" for which we should "glorify God in our bodies and spirits, which are God's" (1 Corinthians 6:20).

And you—in what do you rest your soul? Where is your confidence and rest when adversity knocks at your door? In your status and bank account? And in whom is your hope? In your doctor, your employer, or the profits from your business? Don't misinterpret me; a large bank account, a good job at a respectable company, your own business, and access to the best doctors and health services are great blessings. It is very good to have them and we should value them, but according to David, it is not good to rest in them or put your hope there. Only God should be your rest and your hope. Without God, your bank account, your great position at that company, and your prosperous business can only cause you arguments, envy, and jealousy. And that doctor who is so wise and learned can become your death sentence, because he doesn't know the cure for what ails you. With God, on the other hand, that business and prosperity are to bring His Kingdom and bless you, your loved ones, and the world more, and that sickness can end up in Him being exalted when you are healed. Make an effort, find support in others, plan and protect yourself and your family, but when it comes to trusting, rest only in God, and only let Him be your hope…

> *"Unless the Lord builds the house, they labor in vain who build it; unless the Lord guards the city, the watchman stays awake in vain."*
>
> Psalm 127:1

Prayer: Blessed Holy Spirit, at this moment I choose and receive Your rest. You are my Father, You are powerful and just, and You love me with a love that I cannot even begin to understand. I only find stable and continual peace in You. I let go of all anxiety and relieve myself of all bitterness, complaining, and anxiety. Thank You Lord because I know that I can rest in You.

Day 11: God keeps betting on me

"Behold, the Lord's hand is not shortened, that it cannot save, nor His ear heavy, that it cannot hear. But your iniquities have separated you from your God; and your sins have hidden His face from you, so that He will not hear."

Isaiah 59:1-2

Have you ever wondered, in the middle of anxiety, where God is, and why He doesn't seem to hear your cries or your anguish? Have you felt far away, inaccessible, or unreachable? This quote clarifies that His hand has not been cut short to help you, and His ear hasn't closed so He doesn't hear you. He is where He has always been, near you, waiting for you to change your path and return to Him, to His source. He does not regret having suffered a brutal death to save you, erasing your evil, because He has not renounced you or your return. Jesus keeps waiting on you, believing in you, betting on you, every day, for you to come back to the marvelous path that He designed for you before you were born, and so obtain the brilliant future for which He created you, regardless of your past. He has kept a white stone for you that contains a new name, your true identity (Revelation 2:17). God has not separated Himself from you, which is why He is at your door daily, calling you. If you hear His voice, and open your heart to Him, He will enter into you, and eat with you (will have intimacy according to Revelation 3:20), because no one who comes to Him will be cast out (John 6:37). He is waiting…

However, our sin closes the door in His face. Our rebellion tells Him, "I don't need you, I don't want correction; I don't even believe that You are real or that You love me as much as they say. Get away from my path, I am the owner of my destiny and I control my own steps." Other times, it is our self-esteem that, wounded like a little bird that is crawling, tells Him, "I am a failure, my life is a disaster, there is no way out and no hope for me. I am worthless, so You will never love me or forgive me. If no one visible has loved me, how can I believe in You, when you are invisible?" Satan's same old two strategies: One, to make you believe you are better than everyone, forcing you to build your superiority complex on the columns of your insecurity, and the other made with the bricks of fear of inferiority and reject. Both strongholds don't let the Light in, and must be destroyed…

> *"For the weapons of our warfare are not carnal but mighty in God for pulling down strongholds, casting down arguments and every high thing that exalts itself against the knowledge of God, bringing every though into captivity to the obedience of Christ,"*
>
> 1 Corinthians 10:4-5

Prayer: Holy Lord, today I decide to please You first. I ask for Your Holy Spirit to guide me when pride or self love want to take over me. You love me as I am, but You love me too much to leave me as I am. Thank you, because You are working in my soul.

Day 12: Only He guides my steps

"O Lord, I know the way of man is not in himself; it is not in man who walks to direct his own steps."

Jeremiah 10:23

We live in volatile times, with constant changes and unexpected circumstances, but despite the fact that we are all aware of this reality, we strive to anticipate and plan everything. I have friends with professional career plans that outline the dates and promotions for the next ten years. Each region's culture has established the appropriate age to study, to date, to marry, to have children, to retire, and to become grandparents. If you want to write a book as a child, you are too young, and if you want to study at sixty, you are too old! There is a social pressure that acts like the flow of a river, pushing the majority toward the center of the current, and those who resist the pressure are pushed to the shore, outside. I think that this all comes from a generational fear of losing control and being vulnerable. We live in a world of strength, and it terrifies us to expose our weaknesses to others. Instead of imitating bamboo, which adapts to wind with flexibility, we try to harden ourselves like a heavy boulder that cannot be moved. But boulders do not move with the breeze or grow. Some experts assert that, on average, barely 30% of our day-to-day life can be controlled. What happens if we focus on that small, "controllable" part of our lives? Well, we just lose the other 70%.

Would you tell the captain the best route when you board a cruise ship or a plane? Unless you are a qualified pilot, I would guess not. Then why do you try to do it with your life? Do you know, perhaps, when you will die?

At least do you know when you or your child will fall in love, or the day your wife will have the new baby? If your answer is no, what do you think of giving space for God to work in us? What if we extended our limits and gave room for movement, waiting on His time and not ours, His will and not ours? That is also faith and, what doesn't come from faith is sin (Romans 14:23). Your plans will follow your will and the will of the world that surrounds you. But if you want God's plans in your life, you must live under His will. He has a greater purpose for you, but without His guidance, you will never be able to reach it. Let yourself be guided by the Spirit, the one who gave you your life and orders your steps.

> *"The wind blow where it wishes, and you hear the sound of it, but cannot tell where it comes from and where it goes. So is everyone who is born of the Spirit."*
>
> John 3:8

Prayer: Lord, forgive me because I keep wishing to control my life, living it according to my plans and priorities. Today I give You the wheel, Jesus, and I give you space to work and positively impact my path with Your blessings. You are God, Dad. Only You are God. Thank You, Lord!

Day 13: I love to talk with God

"But you, when you go pray, go into your room, and when you have shut your door, pray to your Father who is in the secret place; and your Father who sees in secret will reward you openly."

Matthew 6: 6

In the same way a doctor gives instructions like taking a medication "with every meal, at bedtime or before going to the bathroom" (because we all eat, sleep, and go to the bathroom), Jesus tells us, "when you pray," meaning it was a given that we do it daily. One cannot be a Christian without praying, daily. Frequent communication and spending time with someone are essential elements of every good relationship, including your relationship with the Holy Spirit. It is good to go to church, help the needy, go to weekly small group meetings and thank God before eating, but none of that is a substitute for prayer (reading the Bible is a form of prayer because He expresses Himself through it).

But unfortunately, for many, the mere idea of enjoying the company and communion of the most marvelous Being who exists, our Creator and Savior, is boring, and is one more burden to bear. How can we think that that pleases God? Just like a mom who tells the misbehaving child, "wait 'til your father comes home, you'll see," religion has created a mentality in us of speaking with "Father" God is a form of penitence, reserved only for those times when we make mistakes.

But a good dad wants much more than to correct his children. To me, at least, it's the part I like least about my relationship with my children.

What I do like is spending time together, listening to their dreams and cultivating them; hugging them, seeing them healthy, watching them grow, giving them my best, providing for them and protecting them. I also exceedingly enjoy sharing individually with my wife or one of my three children. The way they open their heart so I can plant seeds of light, peace, self-esteem, love and courage in it delights me. Just like in your married life, God wants to have secret stories with you from a secret place, adventures that are just between you and Him. That is why He has a language that is just for you, dreams that only you and He understands, surprises that are only yours and indescribable gifts created exactly for the size of your soul. He created your heart to satisfy it with good, and he is going to restore you, transform you, cultivate you, console you, and make you immensely happy. But He needs time alone with you, which is why He urges you to seek it, to crave it, daily, in secret:

> *"God, You are my God; early will I seek You; my soul thirsts for You; my flesh longs for You…"*
>
> Psalm 63:1a

Prayer: My precious Creator, thank You for Your beautiful and sweet availability to be with me. Thank you because even though You are King, High and Lifted Up, You are always there to listen to me, to advise me, to show me Your love. Today I understand that You are real, and what's most beautiful, You want to be my friend…

Day 14: Talking with God transforms me

"Who can understand his errors? Cleanse me from secret faults."
Psalm 19:12

Most believers spend a good portion of their prayer time asking god for what they think they need, despite the fact that Jesus tells us that our heavenly Father knows our needs before we ask Him (Matthew 6:8b). Maybe that is one of the reasons why many people who have been believers for several years have never changed their way of thinking; rather, they keep talking the same way, making the same mistakes, showing the same bad character, the same craftiness, unable to see their own internal conflicts. These people don't pray; they ask, and they repeat prayers and learned phrases (may times designed by other people), without really meditating on them. That is why Jesus warns us about praying with "vain repetitions" or many words (Matthew 6:7). Would you relate to someone who always repeats the same words to you, just asking and asking, and was never remotely interested in listening to you? That would be an exasperating friendship, right? Let's not do the same thing to God!

Prayer time should be the best time of day. If you have a few minutes to speak to the president of your country, would you waste it on irrelevant themes, or would you "squeeze" the most out of it? If you have a daily meeting with God through His Holy Spirit, it is impossible for you not to be transformed, strengthened, restored. When Moses returned from Mount Sinai, he had to cover his face with a veil because it shone after being with God (Exodus 34:35). It is impossible to share quality time every day with the One who created the universe without being renewed. Today, before praying for others, pray for you. Meditate on whether there is any pride hidden in your heart. Perhaps your prayers have centered on your plans and not His, and without meaning to, you are trying to be God. Ask the Father to transform you. Sincerely open the doors of your heart. Like David, ask Him to show you your errors and clean you from them, to bring to mind the limiting paradigms that obstacle you, that stop you from seeing and going further. You will need courage and humility because God is working with you; He will not prune your branches but will go directly to the root; but you can trust in Him, because He loves you. Let the spirit speak to you and pray for you. You don't know what you need, but He does.

> *"Likewise the Spirit also helps in our weaknesses. For we do not know what we should pray for as we ought, but the Spirit Himself makes intercession for us with groanings which cannot be uttered."*
>
> Romans 8:26

Prayer: Father, transform me. I need and want to be renewed, restored. Today I stop playing God and ask You to guide me so my life will be just as You planned. I want to achieve all You created me for. Achieve all the dreams that You put in my heart, in Your way, not in mine, Lord. In Your way...Thank you, Abba.

Day 15: God listens to me, always, and hears my prayers

"You who answer prayer…"

Psalm 65:2

We all know (or sense) that God exists, and that He is omnipresent, omniscient, and omnipotent, and that we were created for Him. As Christians, we also know that Jesus Christ paid the price of our arrogance, that He was handed over for our rebellion and cursed so that we would be blessed. What an incredible expression of His infinite love! However, very few know with certainty, in the deepest part of their being, that God listens to their prayers, all of them, and that even though we can feel far away because of our separation from Him, He is always there, within reach, ready to embrace you, protect you, and care for you and your loved ones. For this reason, He daily tries to attract your attention, but you are so worried about caring for your own issues that you can't discern His Presence or hear His whispers trying to guide you. Would you disregard a friend who sincerely loves you, respects you, is wise, powerful, honest, and trustworthy, and who, on top of it all, only wants your good? I suppose not. However, the Holy Spirit is all that and much more, because He also paid all your debts to free you from evil and death; He died for you… No one has loved you or will ever love you like He has.

You can be absolutely certain of something: God listens and attends to your prayer, because you are more important to Him than anything else. You are His priority. The fact that you don't know His answer doesn't mean that He isn't listening to you. David said, "But certainly God has heard me, He has attended to the voice of my prayer," (Psalm 6:19) and also, "I love the Lord, because He has heard my voice and my supplications. Because He has inclined His ear to me, therefore I will call upon Him as long as I live." (Psalm 116: 1-2) God is not an absent father; rather, He is omnipresent. He does not abandon you and has never hurt you. He doesn't underestimate your pain or ignore the temptations you are going through. The Holy Spirit doesn't ever disregard your prayer, but He is attentive to it. He has not forgotten you; rather, He anxiously seeks your return home. He is quick to attract you, and I believe that every time your heart shows the slightest possibility of calling for Him, He smiles, excited. He holds the hope of a closer relationship with you. He wants to be your first choice, to take care of you. He doesn't like to see you defeated or beaten down but rather well, trusting… God has all that you need and wants to give it to you for your good, but you need to pray and seek Him, knowing that He is there, that although you can't see Him, He is more real than your hands:

> *"Blessed be God, who has not turned away my prayer, nor His mercy from me!"*
>
> Psalm 66:20

Prayer: Today, I understand that You hear my prayer. That when I seek you, I find you because You will always be near. Thank you, because even though I can't see you, my spirit perceives the holiness and presence of Your Spirit. Thank you for always being near, ready for me.

"...that you put off, concerning your former conduct, the old man which grows corrupt according to the deceitful lusts, and be renewed in the spirit of your mind..."
Ephesians 4:22-23

Thank you Father, because Your Word transforms me, daily, and Your love gets the best out of me ...

Day 16: Every day I love my Father more

"Jesus answered and said to him, 'If anyone loves Me, he will keep my word; and My Father will love him, and We will come to him and make Our home with him. He who does not love Me does not keep My words;'"

John 14:23-24a

Marriage is a blessing but demands sacrifices, and if you don't love your spouse enough, you won't do it, to the detriment of the relationship. Spouses can stay together "until death do us part" but perhaps without enjoying true intimacy or genuine companionship. The only way to solve this problem is for one of the spouses to begin to worry more about the other and less about themselves. Something similar occurs in our relationship with God. If you don't sincerely love Him, you will only have a tedious religion, and He will be a burden instead of a blessing to you. On the other hand, we all want our children to obey us and have moral principles but, is this all we expect from them? I want my kids to behave but I also want them to do their very best, to be disciplined and persistent, to choose well, and I also want to enjoy the journey with them, travel together, take their hands and guide them, play with them, kiss them, hug them, protect them, provide for them, and give them good gifts. Although I'm very pleased when they obey and I can even correct them severely depending on the seriousness of each case, I don't love my children because they obey me. I love them because they are mine, because they are marvelous, because God gave them to me, because they were born from my wife and from me. That is what real fatherhood is about, and neither you nor I are better fathers than Papa...

Do you want to receive more of God? Don't worry so much about your morality and about having unimpeachable behavior, but rather spend time with Him. The holiness will come on its own, through the relationship. Do you want to overcome difficulties that block your steps? Don't worry about fighting so much with your faith; spend more time with Him and your faith will grow as you get to know His greatness and His love for you. Do you want to be transformed and leave behind a vice or attachment that only you know about? Seek more of His Presence; the chains of the enemy will fall off when His power descends over you. If you want to receive more of God, you must spend more time with Him so that you can know and love Him more. Only then will you understand His love and passion for you. God wants to give you more, but you must be transformed to be able to receive it… The more you know Him, the more you will love Him.

> *"And you shall love the Lord your God with all your heart, with all your soul, with all your mind, and with all your strength. This is the first commandment."*
>
> Mark 12:30

Prayer: Today I grasp onto You, Lord Jesus. I call You and I know that You respond. Today I understand that I can do nothing apart from You, but I can do all in You because You strengthen me. Today I stop battling sin and I let you fill me, heal me, restore me. Thank You, Daddy. I love you.

Day 17: I have access to Him because he loves me

"Let us therefore come boldly to the throne of grace, that we may obtain mercy and find grace to help in time of need."
                                                              Hebrews 4:16

Recently, my 6-year-old son Daniel, seated on the floor of his "dojang," waited to be called by his teachers to present the test for his orange belt in Tae Kwon Do. I was a little nervous when I saw that he was a little nervous but suddenly, in the middle of the racket of his friends who shouted and pushed one to another, Daniel put his hands together, bowed his head, closed his eyes and prayed, briefly but deeply. I don't know what I felt... I was proud, but of God, of His blessing. My soul was so joyful, because he learned that from me and was spontaneously imitating me, drawing near with a genuine and pure faith to the throne of Grace, to ask for help from his Abba. Suddenly I understood that when we imitate Jesus, who in turn always imitates the Father, our natural and spiritual children imitate us, and we start training part of that chain of generational blessing that comes from Heaven itself, from eternity and for eternity...

Now, if I felt so happy because my young boy son was praying to His Heavenly Father, imagine how the Lord felt! After all, the prayer was for Him, not for me. With the simple act of meditating on this, I now enjoy my prayer time even more, because I imagine that the Father feels something similar to what we feel. God is pleased with you and me, not because we are perfect, but because in our trials, we seek Him and try to imitate Him. And when everything goes well, after overcoming the challenge, we give Him the glory. He always has abundant mercy and grace for us, His children. Jesus isn't watching for your imperfections but your strengths; He doesn't focus on your past but on your potential. God isn't the police, trying to capture you "red handed" to punish you or give you what you deserve. He is more proud of you than you are of your children. What's more, you, just as you are, just as He created you, are a delight to Him. Despite your many defects and fears, with your strengths but also your weaknesses, in your falls and every time you get back up, He is there, available, betting on your success. He is a close Dad, a confidant, the best friend, the Only companion who loves you more than anyone in the universe, so know the best example and learn from Jesus. Imitate the Father...

> *"Then Jesus answered and said to them, 'Most assuredly, I say to you, the Son can do nothing of Himself, but what He sees the Father do; for whatever He does, the Son also does in like manner.'"*

John 5:19

Prayer: Today I will live connected to You. I will not separate myself from Your Holy Spirit. Help me to understand how important I am to you and how you are always there, just for me. Thank You my King for delighting in me. You are incredible!

Day 18: My God wants me to live

"Say to them: 'As I live,' says the Lord God, 'I have no pleasure in the death of the wicked, but that the wicked turn from his way and live. Turn, turn from your evil ways! For why should you die, O house of Israel?'"

Ezekiel 33:11

For many, the God of the Old Testament is a punisher, a harsh and legalistic father who spends His time spying on his children to correct them harshly for the smallest error, but here we see that God is the same in the Old Testament as in the New, and that His love before Christ's sacrifice was equally immense. That's why He sent us the Son. When He says "as I live," He is reinforcing His heart's sincerity to us, showing us His tenderness, as if He were saying "believe me, I'm not tricking you, you have my word." He does not lie, and as such, does not need to validate His Words, but He uses this language to increase our confidence in Him. God does not desire the death of sinners (all of us), but their repentance, that we redirect our path toward Him.

In an act of infinite humility, God laments for those who reject Him and opens His afflicted heart to the prophet, telling Ezekiel something like, "Explain to them that I don't want them to come to me so I can mistreat them or hurt them; on the contrary, what I desire is that they repent so they will live." I don't know what circumstances you have gone through or how far you have fallen while walking in rebellion. I don't know if your mistakes are "like scarlet," but, if you come to Christ, you will be "white as snow" (Isaiah 1:18). The world is sicker and weaker every day, which is why it's urgent to change direction and seek God. But there is an important, and perhaps even more pressing, requirement: understanding that God already loves you infinitely, exactly as you are, with your defects, weaknesses, and virtues. He even loved you since long before you were born. God desires that we return to Him so we will live. If you have given ground to the enemy, granting legal authority over some area of your life to the devil, no matter how hard you try; you will stay trapped until you give yourself up to the Lord. God doesn't condemn you. He came to give you life, and that you would have it more abundantly (John 10:10). He wants to destroy Satan's work that he has built in you, but He can only do that if you invite Him in and let Him work. Don't trust in your good works…

> "*Therefore you, O son of man, say to the children of your people, 'The righteousness of the righteous man shall not deliver him in the day of his transgression; as for the wickedness of the wicked, he shall not fall because of it in the day that he turns from his wickedness; nor shall the righteous be able to live because of his righteousness in the day that he sins.'*"
>
> Ezekiel 33:12

Prayer: Lord, I will not reject you again. Today I understand that you are a Good God and a Good Father, and that all Your commandments and instructions are good for me, for my family and for my descendants. Help me to always walk under Your protection and with Your lamp lighting my steps. Thank You, because I know that You always listen to me and help me.

Day 19: My Father is so humble!

"Now then, we are ambassadors for Christ, as though God were pleading through us; we implore you on Christ's behalf, be reconciled to God."

2 Corinthians 5:20

Have you ever imagined that when someone speaks to you about God, it is the Lord Himself imploring you through him or her? Could it be possible that the person who so insists that you correct your path, leave sin, and sometimes even becomes a little impertinent, is no more than a persistent instrument of God, calling you to return to Him? God frequently speaks to you, but your mind is very distracted with other things, so He sends someone else, speaking to you through others with the hope that you hear His message. If you have a friend or acquaintance whose company you don't always want but, whom you seek out and listen to when you feel emptiness in your soul or when others abandon you, that person is an instrument of God who is begging you to turn back and reconcile with Him. Cultivate that friendship, because the Holy Spirit is behind it.

On the other hand, have you ever considered the possibility that when God moves you to speak about Him to someone, to help someone, or to serve others, it is God Himself pleading with that person to return to Him, through you? And if your heart feels unsettled when you don't do it, or you have an intense desire to dare to do it, then it is God Himself begging you to do it. What a great privilege to be His instrument! How great is the love of the Father, to humble Himself to plead with us to reconcile ourselves to Him! The same One who created us and gave us a beautiful and rich planet to live on; He who gave up His only Son to get us back when we were apart from Him; that same marvelous Creator pleads today for your soul, for mine, and for the soul of millions who, without our intervention, will go an eternity without Christ... God is whispering to us with love today, "Reconcile with me! I am the Way, the Truth and the Life (John 14:6). Come back, turn your steps to Me and I will give you abundant life (John 10:10b). I will not leave you orphans (John 14:18)." If you are in the middle of adversity that seems to deviate you from your path, evaluate and scrutinize it well, because maybe God is returning you to the Way. And if all your issues are going so well that it seems like you don't need Him, examine them, because apart from Him we can do nothing (John 15:5b).

"If My people, who are called by My name will humble themselves, and pray and seek My face, and turn from their wicked ways, then I will hear from heaven, and will forgive their sin and heal their land."

2 Chronicles 7:14

Prayer: Today I humble myself Lord, and I pray and seek your face. I choose to change from my paths to Yours, Father. I want to reconcile myself to You again. Thank you for Your mercy, for Your forgiveness, because you embrace me. I don't want to be apart from You, ever.

Day 20: The "how" is important to my Father

"Unless the Lord builds the house, they labor in vain who build it; unless the Lord guards the city, the watchman stays awake in vain."

Psalm 127:1

A large portion of humanity tries to reach their dreams apart from their Creator, childishly choosing to be an orphan despite the availability of a great Father. In our arrogance, we believe we are independent from that greater Source that we all sense, but do not see... We believe we can reach self-sufficiency, despite the fact that everything that surrounds us is inextricably interconnected and interdependent. The word "vain" could be substituted with "useless" and refer to a sterile effort, like carrying water from the river and spilling it on the path, or following a strict diet and not losing a pound. Here the psalmist teaches us that to live separately from God is useless and senseless, even foolish, like building a boat without a sail, like a river that, without a current, dries up...

God is interested in what you achieve, but even more, in how you get there. It matters a lot to Him how high you climb, but even more, in whose hand you are holding. He's not sitting at the peak, waiting on you, wanting you to get there; rather, He accompanies you for the whole trip, every step, rain or shine, and nourishes you when your face falls. He doesn't only lift you up at your high points. He also cures your wounds when you slip and forgives you tenderly when you make a mistake. But the God's Holy Spirit loves, above all things, your company. You are His greatest delight, His greatest creation, unique, unequalled, perfect. He wants to attract your attention, and for that he paints landscapes around you, with the hopes that you turn to see them, and remember Him. He tries to make you happy with the smiles of those who surround you, to see if you see His reflection. Don't live your life in vain, building walls without cement or watching a city in the dark, chasing after plastic happiness. Don't live without Papa. Don't dismiss His gift or your life. He can, wants to, and will move you forward, if you allow Him. You are not insignificant. You are His special treasure (Malachi 3:17) and his chosen lineage (1 Peter 2:9). Don't get lost in the shadows; you can be really free, but only with His help. It doesn't matter how desperate your situation seems; there is an exit, there is a solution. Have hope, and that hope has a name: Jesus Christ. Only in Him. Don't leave the source; stay on the vine.

> Jesus Christ said, *"I am the vine, you are the branches. He who abides in Me, and I in him, bears much fruit; for without Me you can do nothing."*
>
> John 15:5

Prayer: Today, I renounce being an orphan, because I know that I have a faithful, loving, and powerful Father in Heaven. Holy Spirit, today I want to invite you to permeate all aspects of my life. I want you to be with me in the office, in my daily routines, in traffic, eating, bathing, getting up, and going to bed. I want to live close to You, Holy Lord. Thank You.

Day 21: Today I meditate on His ways

"You have sown much, and bring in little; you eat, but do not have enough; you drink, but you are not filled with drink; you clothe yourselves, but no one is warm; and he who earns wages, earns wages to put into a bag with holes." Thus says the Lord of hosts: 'Consider your ways!'"

Haggai 1:6-7

Despite the unlimited amount of advertisements for different toys that promise to make us happier, more satisfied, thinner, more muscular, more spiritual, sexier, more intellectual, more emotional, more creative and professional, better fathers, better lovers and better leaders, always enjoying (of course) economic abundance and "mental peace," I believe that humanity is divided in two unique groups: those who have found their reason to exist and those who haven't. And I believe that only the second group needs all these toys. The world's happiness seems inversely proportional to the richness and technological resources available. We seek happiness through well-trodden paths, even though we see the unhappiness of those who have gone before us. But if happiness is the path, shortcuts only shorten and reduce it!

Is there vanity in your life? I'm not referring to arrogance, but to effort in vain. Do you eat without being satisfied, dress yourself but never get warm, and put your wages in a torn bag? If so, listen to the prophet's instructions: "Consider your ways." It doesn't matter how many paths there seem to be, each one leads to a different place.

Where do you want to end up: Do you want the shortcut, or would you rather walk? God has placed a route inside of you that only you can travel, with the exact imprint of your feet and extra space for your biggest dreams; specialized to develop your gifts and specifically designed for you to need His companionship for the whole journey, because His greatest pleasure is to walk with you. "Consider your ways." Don't go where everyone else goes if you want to get to a different place. Don't walk on the beaten bath if you're looking for something better than what the average person seeks. Don't push all the doors open without knowing what lies behind them; instead, let your Father be a gentleman and open them for you, if they are good for you... Be all that you were created for. Don't follow anyone blindly, even God. Meditate on His ways, every day, in every decision. Choose the good and the light, because although the paths seem the same, the destinations could be very different...

> *"Because narrow is the gate and difficult is the way which leads to life, and there are few who find it."*
>
> Matthew 7:14

Prayer: Lord, today I ask You for forgiveness for the times that I have wanted to live my way, following the world's idea of success, trying to reach standards set by people that I don't even know. Today I ask you to help me live according to Your will, so that my life will be truly productive. Thank You.

Day 22: I am thankful

"And you shall love the Lord your God with all your heart, with all your soul, with all your mind, and with all your strength. This is the first commandment."

Matthew 12:30

When did I lose the ability to be amazed and stop perceiving each day's miracles? When was it that I stopped nourishing my soul, and why didn't I realize it was so malnourished? How did I not realize the marvel of being one flesh with my wife, enjoying my children, and how fabulous it is to breathe, laugh, cry…? In spite of millions of different hues, my eyes insist on black and white; with so much love all around, I focus on where it's lacking. How did I start dismissing the treasure of every minute, living as if I were never going to die, while I abandoned my dreams, as if I were already dead? Is the birth of a baby less marvelous because one happens every few seconds? Shouldn't I be left breathless by the full moon, a sunset, or because of Christ's open arms on the Cross, embracing me as well? How did I learn to pay attention to what I lack and not what I have, when I have so much? Why did I assume that my resources belonged to me and that I deserve everything I receive? Where was it that I learned the illusion of possession? What is really mine? When and how did I become so insensitive and arrogant?

Blessed Creator: Teach me to love You with all my being! Let my soul, my mind and my strength be Yours. Forgive me for becoming accustomed to living life as if it belonged to me, as if I had given it to myself. Forgive me for assuming, every night, that my eyes would open back up in the morning and that Your breath would be in my mouth. Forgive my speech; it's always me, me, me, as if the universe revolved around me... Transform me! Wake me up! Teach me to be realistic, meaning to live "Your reality" instead of my ignorance. Open my soul so that I can finally understand that life is marvelous and is Your gift, which comes only from You, because You sustain the universe with the power of Your Word (Hebrews 1:3). I don't want to dismiss You anymore. I want to change; I don't want to be a spoiled child. I am so sorry for having thrown aside so many gifts, without even opening them, Jesus! Help me, Holy Spirit, to live on a higher frequency, with a humble heart, more awake to You and Your will, and less sensitive to the tricks of this world. Starting right now, I will be thankful, and like David,

> *"I will bless the Lord at all times; His praise shall continually be in my mouth."*
>
> Psalm 34:1

Prayer: Father, help me to live deeper than the surface. Let me perceive more of You, have a more significant, more transcendent life, according to the plans in Your heart when You created me, when you designed me, when you saved me. Father, guide me so my life will have meaning, so Your sacrifice will be worth it. I love you, Abba.

Day 23: Today I open my mind to His goodness

"Now I say that the heir, as long as he is a child, does not differ at all from a slave, though he is master of all,"

Galatians 4:1

According to Paul, it is possible that, although someone governs (is master) all and as such is the owner of all, he can live the life of a slave. I believe that some Hollywood celebrities are a good example of this: lives full of blessing (beauty, talent, and economic abundance) and misery at the same time (greed, envy, gossip, adultery, divorce, abandoned children). Rather than take ownership of the blessing they have, the blessing owns them. How is it possible for someone to have "everything" and nothing at the same time? Immaturity. A child doesn't have the mental or legal capacity to make decisions about his or her own inheritance, and unfortunately, neither do many believers...

Most of God's children live far below their potential. They get scattered blessings, but at the cost of a lot of dissatisfaction and frustration. Their character limits them because they don't allow the Holy Spirit to transform them, so they spend months and years stuck, not evolving; squandering the power, eternal life, and Grace that God generously provides them, as if it were something common and worthless. Unfortunately, many are used to living like the woman who "was bent over and could in no way raise herself up," (Luke 13:11) who, despite her unfortunate condition and having heard the testimonies of Jesus' miracles, did not ask the Master to heal her when He went to preach in her own synagogue; or the paralytic who had been immobile for thirty-eight years. When Jesus asked him, "Do you want to be made well?" instead of shouting a clear and forceful "Yes, I want to walk, I want to be free," he started giving Jesus all the explanations for why "his case" had no solution and he couldn't be cured (John 5:6-7). What a waste of time and life, having the One who is the Fullness of God in front of him! (Colossians 2:9). Don't get accustomed to living bent over; don't let your mind paralyze you. Don't stop growing in God. Meditate on His Word, adore Him and pray to Him daily. Let Him transform you through the renewing of your mind (Romans 12:2) so that you reach maturity in Him and can thus enjoy all the blessings that He has given you as His coheir, like His Son, not like a child or a slave:

"Therefore you are no longer a slave but a son, and if a son, then an heir of God through Christ."

Galatians 4:7

Prayer: Today I renounce all forms of slavery in the world. Thank you because You and only You are my Lord. I'm thankful for all You do for me, and I treasure Your Word and Your anointing Lord. There is no good for me apart from You, Jesus. I love you…

Day 24: Today I rely on His mercy

"And while he lingered, the men took hold of his hand, his wife's hand, and the hands of his two daughters, the Lord being merciful to him, and they brought him out and set him outside the city."

Genesis 19:16

The gentlemen were angels who appeared as men (Hebrews 13:2) who came to take Lot (Abraham's nephew) and his family out of Sodom. God wanted to save their lives, because destruction was imminent. This city was known for the perversion of all its inhabitants ("both old and young," Genesis 19:4), who were so depraved that they tried to sexually abuse the visitors (angels) who visited Lot (Genesis 19:5-9). But God's messengers, because of their rush to protect Lot and his family from extermination: "took hold of his [Lot's] hand, his wife's hand, and the hands of his two daughters, the Lord being merciful to him." The angels literally grabbed the hands of those chosen by God to protect them and free them, according to His mercy. They must not be destroyed like the rest of the people of this city. God applied His wrath while he protected His children.

If you are going through a difficult situation at this moment, whether it's a personal or professional challenge, an illness, economic scarcity or deep emotional disappointment, remember that God, "being merciful," takes your hand and doesn't let it go, even though you can't feel it. Jesus says of us, His sheep, that "… no one is able to snatch them out of my Father's hand." (John 10:29b) He promised that He would always be there. In difficulties, He makes himself more real and tangible, but you need to believe Him and take the time to seek Him. And if it's a loved one who is confronting problems, there is more good news here: the angels protected them, being merciful to him, not to his wife and daughters so, if you love God and seek Him and believe Him, He will hear your intercession and free others, "being merciful to you." What's more, it all started with Abraham who was "the friend of God" (James 2:23), and that's why the angels freed Lot, because of his uncle's (Abraham's) intercession (Genesis 18). Let's seek God's friendship, and He will hear our intercession from Heaven, and those who surround you will be blessed as well. Only this way we can change the world...

"Yet the Lord would not destroy Judah, for the sake of His servant David, as He promised him to give a lamp to him and his sons forever."

2 Kings 8:19

Prayer: Thank you, blessed Holy Spirit, because even though I can't feel Your hand, it sustains me, me and mine, day and night. Your mercy is never far from me. Bless You, Lord.

Day 25: Today I know that He has received me

"All that the Father gives Me will come to Me, and the one who comes to Me I will by no means cast out."

John 6:37

Jesus establishes several vital principles for our faith here: First: Father God is Jesus's provider, and for that matter, ours; it is He who provides the souls and resources for His Kingdom. That's why David said, "My goodness is nothing apart from You," (Psalm 16:2c), and John the Baptist, "…A man can receive nothing unless it has been given to him from heaven." (John 3:27) Second: The fact that even if you can't touch what God has promised you with your hands, that doesn't mean it isn't yours. Jesus gives us the example, receiving in the present ("gives me") what the Father will later give Him ("will come to me"). Jesus's faith rests on the One who is His source. The intimacy between them doesn't leave room for doubt. He knows He owns everything that still hasn't happened or that hasn't even been started. You are already the receiver of all that God has promised you; it's just a matter of time for it to be manifested, because, in His time, what He already gave you "will come to you."

Third: It is God who attracts souls, not us. That's why He says "the one who comes to Me," so we shouldn't waste time on profane and idle babblings (2 Timothy 2:16). Don't scramble to convince people about Jesus's existence. Talk less and listen more, try to understand and have a good testimony. Don't argue with those who you would like to see at His feet. Pray for them, alone. Bend your knees for their souls. Call out to the Father in your daily intimacy with Him. Fourth: The mistakes that you have made or that have been made against you don't matter, and neither does how wrong your past has been. It doesn't matter how deep is the hole you have buried yourself or how thick the swamp where you wallowed. The size of the wound you caused or received doesn't matter either. The only thing that matters is that Jesus Christ doesn't cast you out. Ever! If you are really repentant of your sins, He is always available to forgive you, heal you, restore you and lift you up. It's not too late. You still have time; right now is the moment. Don't wait any longer. That's why He died on a cross, so that you would return to Him. His love for you and me is incomprehensible, but even though you don't understand it, don't dismiss it.

> *"Who forgives all your iniquities, Who heals all your diseases, Who redeems your life from destruction, Who crowns you with loving kindness and tender mercies,"*
>
> Psalm 103:3-4

Prayer: Lord, I don't have words to thank You for Your sovereign and absolute forgiveness. You have forgiven all my iniquities and have forgotten each of them. Today you erase all my evil and write my name in the Book of Life. I have no words, Lord. I can only say thank You!

Day 26: He is my Healer

"Behold, I will bring it health and healing; I will heal them and reveal to them the abundance of peace and truth."

Jeremiah 33:6

God promises that He will restore the people of Israel after captivity, but in a broader sense, we gentiles have also been made the people of God through Jesus Christ. Therefore, this promise is also for us, but we need to take ownership of it. That's why Jesus healed everyone: Jews, Romans, Samaritans, Greeks, poor or rich, blind or deaf, paralytic or with leprosy, men and women, sick in body, sick in soul and sick in spirit... And in the most extreme case, when it seemed that the Master had gotten there too late, He then raised the dead. There are no limits to His power, and limits to His love for you don't exist, either. You only have to take hold of His goodness, His grace, His eternal life. He loves you so much that He didn't even spare His own Son (Romans 8:32) to give you complete, good, abundant life. Don't keep doubting or putting Him to the test. He already gave Himself up for you.

The Bible asserts that we were created in the image of God (Genesis 1:27), and Paul says that we are three in one: spirit, soul and body (1 Thessalonians 5:23), three manifestations of the same being, like God (Father, Son and Holy Spirit). That's why we see some illnesses that show up in the body but have a psychological (from the soul) origin, like asthma or depression. Others are perceived in the psyche but their root is spiritual, like all of those who were bound that Jesus freed. I don't know what type of illness you may be suffering through today: a tumor, depression, or allergy. Maybe you have a lot of pain in your bones, you are losing your vision or you suffer from impotence or frigidity, or maybe you have a lot of rage, frustration, anxiety or continuous tiredness. It might not be you, but one of your most loved ones, but God doesn't just want to heal you today. He wants to reveal an abundance of peace and an abundance of His truth to you. And I want to invite you to grasp onto that promise, to hold on with all of your spirit to His Spirit. To declare, wait, and anticipate health, medicine, cure. Declare it, confess it, believe it until you feel "the abundance of peace and truth." He can and wants to do it, but you must believe it with every fiber of your being, with every thought, every blink, every breath. After all, the health that you need is not new or difficult for Him:

> *"When evening had come, they brought to Him many who were demon-possessed. And He cast out the spirits with a word, and healed all who were sick."*
>
> Matthew 8:16

Prayer: Powerful Lord, heal me, save me, free me. I call out for Your precious Blood to come over my spirit, my soul, and my body. You heal all my sicknesses, and all oppression, pain and spirit of sickness flees from me now, in the Name of Jesus. Thank you, because it is already done.

Day 27: I need Jesus's touch

"a man who was full of leprosy saw Jesus; and he fell on his face and implored Him, saying, 'Lord, if You are willing, You can make me clean.' Then He put out His hand and touched him, saying, 'I am willing; be cleansed.' Immediately the leprosy left him."

Luke 5:12b-13

This leprous man didn't mind putting his mistreated face on the dry ground to prostrate himself before Jesus and make a beautiful plea, "if You are willing, You can make me clean." There are two things that exceedingly impact me about this man's faith. First, the fact that he didn't say, "if You can;" rather, he said, "if You are willing." He was sick and surely suffered strong social rejection, but he also knew that Jesus had the power to heal him (make him clean) completely. Second, he didn't ask the Lord the question, "Do you want to clean me?" Instead, he made an affirmation, a declaration of faith in Jesus, "[I know that] if You are willing, You can make me clean." Surely this man with leprosy, like all the rest in his time, carried a bell that rang while he walked to warn everyone to get away from the unpleasant spectacle, an "unclean" was coming near (Leviticus 13:8) and, according to the law, if anyone touched him or even made contact with something he touched, they would be equally unclean. Jesus's answer didn't make him wait, and it demonstrates His love and supernatural power. Although He could have healed him without touching him (not making Himself unclean according to the law), He intentionally "put out His hand and touched him, saying, I am willing; be cleansed." Then something marvelous happened: Jesus didn't become unclean; instead, the leprous man was restored.

Do you sometimes feel like something is "unclean" in your heart? Maybe it's because of something you did, or on the other hand, was done to you; or you committed a serious error or someone abused you, and just the memory of that situation causes frustration, hate and shame. Maybe a severe addiction has separated you from those you love; maybe a financial, professional or marital failure stays thrust like an arrow in your soul, and causes you still more pain to try to take it out. It could be that you have gone far from God because you think you are unworthy of Him, but I have good news: Jesus can and wants to make you clean, now. Not because of your dignity, but because of His. Right now, seek a place where you are alone, and just like this man, prostrate yourself and sincerely say, "Lord, if You are willing, You can make me clean." I know He will touch you, and His words will also resound in the depths of your soul: "I am willing; be cleansed."

> *"You are already clean because of the word which I have spoken to you."*
>
> Jesus in John 15:3

Prayer: Blessed Jesus Christ, I receive Your cleaning and health now, in the Name of Jesus. I receive Your health in my body and soul. All pain, all disease, all oppression, all anxiety and depression go away, in Jesus's Name. Thank You because I know that You hear my prayer.

Day 28: Today I boast in Him

"My soul shall make its boast in the Lord; the humble shall hear of it, and be glad."

Psalm 34:2

When I think about the fact that not only I can love my family but I can also delight in that love because I can see my children play (thanks to the fact that I have eyes), I can embrace my wife and kiss her (because I have arms and a mouth), and I can even provide for them thanks to health, work and the life that God puts in us. When I speak to someone and feel that God is speaking through me, and I see that person's life transformed by the power and love of the Holy Spirit. When I see how every past difficulty has been preparation for a present blessing. When I remember how God has brought us to different places, and we have found grace and favor in each one, with friends who are like siblings. When I see the rainbow in the ever-changing clouds, or a fish in a pond; with all these things, I can do nothing but give thanks and thanks and more thanks to Jesus, because He has been so generous, so selfless, so sweet and so protective. Father and friend, mentor and brother, who comforts me and also challenges me, who protects me but pushes me forward, the Lamb and the Lion. This is why a thankful David said, "my goodness is nothing apart from You" (Psalm 16:2b).

It's very recommendable that you seek God when your projects turn out bad, but whom do you seek when your plans prosper and bloom, when everything goes well? Today I unite with the Psalmist and invite you, in every circumstance, good or bad, success or failure, peace or trials, at the summit or in the pit, in your comfort zone or being stretched, to boast only in God. For example, if your work is all about you, your ability, and the successes that you have achieved, look for a way to shift that glory to God. Is there an abundance of goods in your house? Then boast in your provider. Do you have a healthy family? Boast in God. Many do not. He is the root of all good. It's great that you have abilities, but who gave you that intelligence? You have many gifts, but where do they come from? He put them inside of you since you were in your mother's womb (Psalm 139:13). Look and see how the Word is true: When someone recognizes that all good comes from God and boasts in him, rebels and self-sufficient people are annoyed, because it hurts their egos. But the humble, free from haughtiness and arrogance, they "are glad." That's the difference between the believer and the unbeliever: obedience and not rebellion, humility instead of arrogance, Him first instead of me first. Which is why John the Baptist said,

> "He [Jesus] *must increase, but I must decrease."*
>
> John 3:30

Prayer: Holy Father, today I take inventory of every blessing, and I take a minute to give You thanks. I know that every good thing in my life has only one origin: You.

Day 29: Today I seek God, and I find Him

"And you will seek Me and find Me, when you search for Me with all your heart."

Jeremiah 29:13

God is not a religion who is found through rituals or a list of moral instructions created to differentiate between the good and the bad. Those who invented religions and those who follow them simply don't know; they suppose. They think about a far-off entity instead of a nearby Father, an ethereal being and not the One who gave Himself up for love. They think of a force that is powerful but without feelings. But here we see that even before Jesus's sacrifice to reconnect us to the Father, the Lord has desired for you and me to seek Him. He wants to be found, because His love for us is infinite. The Holy Spirit wants us to have communion with Him; He wants a relationship, friendship, nearness, and not just requests and complaints. He is not just a God of Sundays, of when we are scared or when we have no other option. We should try to know Him, desire Him, and always seek Him "with all our heart."

God is not impressed with our works of charity or our morals, with our vain words, with the many times that we flippantly say "God bless you," or for prayers mumbled like mantras while our mind is focused on something else. He wants our mind, our heart, our will and strength (Mark 12:30). He created you and gave His precious life for you and me, risking it all, sacrificing it all; therefore He is worthy for us to love Him, seek Him, and know Him, and only when that happens will we find Him. I love that about Jesus. You can't trick or manipulate Him, or make Him feel sorry for you. The Lord knows your potential and knows that you can do great things so, your complaints and excuses don't move Him to intervene. He will never just say, "poor little you." God trusts you and knows that with His help, you can always move forward, and vice versa, without His help, you cannot ("… for without Me you can do nothing." John 15:5). God knows exactly what is in your heart, and if you don't seek Him with sincere desire ("with all your heart"), you simply will not find Him. With God there are no shortcuts, and He hates hypocrisy, so start loving Him right now, exalting His name and thanking Him for all the things that only He has given and granted you, most of them before you knew.

> *"For this says the Lord to the house of Israel: 'Seek Me and live;'"*
> Amos 5:4

Prayer: Today I seek You and desire You. Today I know that You are real, Lord. Today I seek You with all my heart…Thank You, because You always let me find You.

Day 30: Today I praise my Creator

"Thus says the Lord: 'Let not the wise man glory in his wisdom, let not the mighty man glory in his might, nor the rich man glory in his riches; but let him who glories glory in this, that he understands and knows me…'"

Jeremiah 9:23-24a

It is good to be wise, courageous or rich if you understand that it doesn't come from your own hand but that God is the one who granted it to you. Abundance of all goods is a good thing, if you understand that it's on loan, and you should use it appropriately. We live in a world where vanity is seen as virtue and arrogance as self-confidence, although biblically, both are rebellion. That's why we see the athlete who beats his chest while he screams with primitive boasting after scoring, and we see musicians or actors be literally "adored" while they pose, immobile like statues, for their admirers. I don't believe success and fame are bad. On the contrary, they allow for influence over other people and future generations. But the self-importance of the one who says "I did all this, by myself, with my own strength and abilities," takes glory from the One who created you, He who was the one who put those talents in your soul and caused you to be born at a certain place and in certain circumstances. He planned you long before you were born (Isaiah 43:7).

God is searching for thankful hearts that really recognize and understand that while their own effort helped them reach success, it was God who laid the groundwork, planted the seed, and has accompanied them in the process, watering it. How good that you are intelligent, but where did that gift come from? It's extraordinary that you are able to do great things but, did you choose those qualities or were they given to you? That's why the Lord says here not to boast in what you have, but in the fact that you understand and know the One who gave it to you. If you are going to boast, do it based on your relationship with the One who created you. Today, God says to you, "Do you want to be wise, courageous and rich? Understand Me (read My Word) and know Me (seek My Presence), and only then boast, but boast in Me, in that you know Me and understand Me, in that we enjoy a sweet friendship, in the fact that you know that only I Am your Creator and there is no one else before Me. I am your Redeemer, your God; your One and sufficient Lord, your Abba Father." Testimony, testimony, testimony…

> *"But 'he who glories, let him glory in the Lord;' for not he who commends himself is approved, but whom the Lord commends."*
>
> 1 Corinthians 10:17-18

Prayer: Abba, although it sounds a little strange, today I glory in You. I want to be able to know You more, learn more of You, be transformed to be able to boast but not in myself, in You. You are marvelous. Thank You Lord.

"I am the vine, you are the branches. He who abides in Me, and I in him, bears much fruit; for without Me you can do nothing."
John 15:5

Father, only You renew the branches of my soul. Make me sprout, bloom, and bear fruit ...

Day 31: I treasure your commands

"You shall not make for yourself a carved image—any likeness of anything that is in heaven above, or that is in the earth beneath, or that is in the water under the earth;"

Deuteronomy 5:8

The commandments are warnings, not threats. When you order your child not to play ball on the sidewalk of a high-traffic street, it isn't to take away the pleasure of playing but to protect (and probably save) his life. When you instruct a teenager not to drink alcohol or to use a good amount of moderation, you aren't repressing him, you are protecting and avoiding a potential addiction. God loves you so much that He didn't just create you; rather, He bought you, with His own life. We should see the commandments free of religious rigidities that only find punishment and condemnation everywhere. Every good father gives limits to his children through instructions and rules, not to satisfy his ego or to feel superior, but for their good.

After humanity's spiritual fall in the Garden of Eden, spiritual death came, and we lost communion with God, which is why now we can only perceive the natural, although we all sense that one more real and eternal world. The access to the spiritual world (that Adam and Moses, among others, enjoyed) was closed because of humanity's rebellion.

That's why human beings commonly seek to represent God visibly, to physically touch Him and physically conceive what is ethereal and invisible, but when you make an image of God you don't offend Him;

you limit Him. The command in the verse continues: "...you shall not bow down to them nor serve them. For I, the Lord your God, am a jealous God..." (verse 9). It's not about God feeling insecure and needing to control us or dominate us to feel calm. He refers to His desperate desire to bless us and care for us. I don't know how you would feel, but I would be sad if my children, in the middle of a problem, sought help from a neighbor instead of from me. Can this neighbor possibly love them more or comfort them better than I? I don't think so. God also knows that only He can move us forward, that only He Himself is the Way, the Truth, and the Life (John 14:6) and that without Him we are lost and can do nothing (John 15:5). His jealousy comes when the precious life that He gave us is under threat of destruction because of our ignorance, and we don't allow Him to act to help us. God loves you; open the curtains and let His light brighten you:

> *"Or do you think that the Scripture says in vain, 'The Spirit who dwells in us yearns jealously?"*
>
> James 4:5

Prayer: Today I get rid of every form of idolatry Lord Jesus. Today I renounce saddening Your soul by trusting in idols that cannot help me. Today I seek You alone. Thank you for loving me jealously.

Day 32: There is eternity within me

"He has made everything beautiful in its time. Also He has put eternity in their hearts, except that no one can find out the work that God does from beginning to end."

Ecclesiastes 3:11

Your heart perceives eternity because it's inside it. Something in your soul knows, with certainty, that you will never die, and like the puppy who gets excited when the owner pays attention to it, your spirit gets excited and inspired when you take time and scratch a little deeper… For example, butterflies abound in many places, but something happens when you take the time to look specifically at one, up close. A small door to your eternity opens up. The same happens with a sunrise or a starry sky. When you focus all your attention, the next level of existence opens for you. Silently watch your children while they play in the park. If you focus, you will see that they are much more than little beings that laugh and shout. They have eternity, the same life of God, living in them. A musical scale, a mathematical formula, a Bible verse—they are all little keys that open doors to the immense eternity that dwells in your heart. But you need to meditate, pay attention, see beyond the obvious. Jesus Christ taught us this principle, which is why when He finished His deep (although simple at first glance) parables, He declared, "He who has ears to hear, let him hear," (Matthew 13:9).

Don't stay on the surface. There are many manifestations of God's greatness, hidden in daily life. Jesus gave the example: He in whom all the fullness of the Godhead dwells (Colossians 2:9) was, at first sight, a simple carpenter so, the teachers of the law who daily studied about Him, who argued about what the Messiah would be like and gave prophecies about the date of His coming, couldn't recognize Him. Like someone who looks for glasses that he is wearing, they were too occupied with what they were waiting for, with the visible and apparent, and not with the real. That's why they couldn't detect it. They were more focused on the frame than the canvas it contained. That's why "superficial" people are more unhappy and empty, even when they have success, fame, power, and riches. Nothing really valuable is obtained by living only on the external level of your existence, because God has put eternity inside of you. Remember that your citizenship is not on Earth but in Heaven (Philippians 3:20). He put a glorious and unique plan in your soul that will only start to be revealed when you are awake to His greatness. Get rid of banal distractions and focus on Him. God planned it so:

"Seek and you will find." Matthew 7:7

Prayer: Lord, teach me to see through Your eyes. I want to see what You see. I want what hurts You to hurt me and to rejoice in what makes You glad. Open my eyes, my ears. I want to understand you, Papa. Thank you so much!

Day 33: There is eternity within me

"He has made everything beautiful in its time. Also He has put eternity in their hearts, except that no one can find out the work that God does from beginning to end."

Ecclesiastes 3:11

The book of Genesis says Adam and Eve were created in God's image. I believe one of our divine characteristics most similar to the Father is the seed of eternity that He has put in our hearts. At least in the natural, earthly world, only human beings have this ability, but just like a seed kept in a bag or abandoned in a drawer, although it has life within it, it cannot grow. All too often, our eternity stays hidden, atrophied, without "taking root," but that doesn't mean it doesn't exist. The essence is still there, waiting for you to water it and take it out into the sunlight. And it will wait there while you live. Don't wait any more!

There is no more relevant question for your life than this: what does God want to do with me? I have spoken with people close to death, and none of them are interested in the superficial or material. None were comforted in the goods that they earned or the brand of suit that they once wore. What they crave is more time—time to love, time to give to others and to do really important things, like a hug, a bike ride or going fishing. Is there anything more relevant than giving and receiving love? These people wish they had lived a more transcendent, relevant life, an end full of satisfaction, a true achievement, not something superficial. The lost time hurts them so much, and they would give anything to get it back. It seems that only in that moment do we realize that we brought nothing, and we will take nothing with us. We should be sensitive to the voice of that eternity that God put in each of us, in every heart, without exception. Let's learn to listen to the Holy Spirit's voice while we observe the "banal" events of every day, to be able to evaluate them through His lens. What would you worry about if you were going to die today? Don't lose more time, distracted by flashes, craving food where none exists and for breath where there is none. Live one day at a time, focused on Christ. Meditate on how much blessing you give, how much good you do, how you can be better, how you could give more, and so perceive even more of His glory. Leave the surface now, dive in to the deep, and submerge yourself in God, because nothing that you think you have belongs to you:

> *"For we brought nothing into this world, and it is certain we can carry nothing out."*
>
> 1 Timothy 6:7

Prayer: Father, I want to be truthful, real, authentic, exactly how You created me, to achieve all You created me for, according to the way You planned it. Take away all my vanity, arrogance, and superficiality, forever. Clean me, Lord Jesus!

Day 34: There is eternity within me

"Then He got into one of the boats, which was Simon's and asked him to put out a little from the land. And He sat down and taught the multitudes from the boat."

Luke 5:3

The boat is Simon's (Peter's) source of income and main business activity, but the Lord doesn't want to use it just to fish but rather to preach, and that's why He asks them to put out a little from the land, from the earthly, temporal. God wants everything in our life to have His fingerprint imprinted on it and be governed by the spiritual, which is why Philippians tells us to pray without ceasing. You are not a body with a soul; rather, you are a spirit who lives in your body, interconnected through your soul (psyche). Your real you, is invisible on Earth, and God created it with a plan that began long before, and will go on long after your physical life. Paul explains that our being is "spirit, soul and body," (1 Thessalonians 5:23) in that order, so defining the hierarchy and preponderance of the spiritual over the natural, which is why some call the spiritual world supernatural. Jesus also said that what we bind on earth will be bound in Heaven, so there is a correlation between both spheres; you cannot act in one without affecting the other…

Your work or business plays a key role in the plan for your life, but neither those nor your riches are the objective of that plan. Rather, they are the means and resources to carry it out. Your plan is spiritual, but it is executed through your bodily manifestation. Moses lived in Pharaoh's palace so that he would later have access to him, and he had to live in the desert to be able to guide the people there. God did not put him there for so many years to punish him, but to turn him into a powerful prophet. Joseph, for his part, surely learned to speak Egyptian while he was Potiphar's slave, and in jail he learned the kingdom's culture. In adversity, God prepared him to govern Egypt. The challenges that he faced weren't to hurt him, but to promote him. John the Baptist was born when his parents were old because only then was the time to announce Jesus. His parents' long wait had a profound meaning that would only later be revealed. After preaching, the Lord invited a tired Peter to fish again, and now the net was full of so many fish that he had to ask for the help of another boat, and share. If you are in His plan, your life will be a blessing to others. Like Peter, God begs you today to loan him your boat and put out from the land, hear His Word, and only then, go fishing...

> *"But seek first the kingdom of God and His righteousness, and all these things shall be added to you."*
>
> Matthew 6:33

Prayer: Holy Spirit, I want you to be my priority every minute of every day. Today I understand that you have specific plans for me, so I won't compare myself with anyone, and I wait patiently for my opportunities while I live in awareness of Your guidance. I bless you Jesus of Nazareth. Thank You for every drop of Your precious blood.

Day 35: Today I focus on what is really important

"Because: all flesh is as grass, and all the glory of man as the flower of the grass. The grass withers, and its flower falls away,"
1 Peter 1:24

Once, when I faced an intense difficulty, someone suggested that I declare and repeat to myself: "this too shall pass." I believe that is wise and very powerful advice, because in the middle of the desert we see everything so dry, and when facing desperation, we forget that God has always been with us and has never failed us. But what about living a little more aware of what we all know but most seem to ignore: that our life will also pass? We are so interested in the image that we adopt to protect our vulnerability before the world that we come to believe it is real, confusing illusion with our divinity; so worried about earthly promises that we forget the heavenly ones; so distracted worshiping the success the world offers that we forget the eternal and let the seed of arrogance take root in our hearts, silencing and postponing the most important question: where did we come from, and where are we going?

It doesn't matter what we do; our glory will pass. I am not proposing that you don't try or abandon your goals, but that you broaden them a little more, to eternity. When I am anxious about worries of the day to day, I ask myself, what impact will this have in ten years? Does this tension make sense? For whose glory am I working? Why so much stress on what is temporary and so much anxiety in what is only dust? You are much more than this mask called personality. You are more than your fame, your image, or your physical appearance. You are not your bank account, and no matter how much power you have or how much fear you can instill, you too will pass! You are not the body that you see in the mirror, but the eternal spirit who temporary lives in it, and no matter how good you look today, it too shall pass! Only Jesus Christ is "the brightness of His glory and the express image of His person, and upholding all things by the word of His power" (Hebrews 1:3). Only in Jesus Christ do we have transcendence, eternity, salvation and abundant life. Don't worry so much about temporary things. Work less for your plans and your "kingdom" and make more effort for His; less for your glory and more for His. Relax, rest in Him. Only He is worthy, powerful, and eternal. Glory yes, but in the Lord:

> *"But he who glories, let him glory in the Lord; for not he who commends himself is approved, but whom the Lord commends."*
> 2 Corinthians 10:17-18

Prayer: Lord, I want to expand my mind. I want to leave the banal and stop living in the irrelevant, to become all that You, with infinite love, created me for. I don't want to let You down; I don't want to let me down. Inspire me, Papa.

Day 36: I do all that You want

"And when He had removed him, He raised up for them David as king, to whom also He gave testimony and said, 'I have found David the son of Jesse, a man after My own heart, who will do all my will.'"

Acts 13:22

God says something impressive here about David: "He is a man after My own heart. His heart operates and feels like Mine. He is pleased, happy, and hurt by the same things as Me." Isn't that incredible? How can a human being, who has committed serious sins, including sexual abuse and murder, have a heart similar to God's? The same verse gives the answer—because of his obedience: "who will do all My will." God doesn't just want to achieve great things with you. He wants you to want to do it, and to enjoy it. He doesn't just want you to be faithful to your wife, but that you also appreciate what that means and are happy to do it. It's not a matter of just not stealing, but that you are happy with what you have and don't harbor envy in your soul when your neighbor gets richer, because only God is your provider. The Lord isn't recognizing David for having perfect morals, his religion, or even for his works of charity; rather, from so much deep communion, the son's heart starts to look like the Father's. Let's see:

When Saul started suffering attacks from a distressing spirit from God (1 Samuel 16:14-15), they called David to calm him by playing the harp. The report that the king's servant gave about David was this:

"… [David] is skillful in playing, a mighty man of valor, a man of war, prudent in speech, and a handsome person; and the Lord is with him" (verse 18). He was a musician and poet (psalmist), but a man of war; a mighty man, but prudent in his words; handsome but valiant. The perfect man for every woman, the envy of every man, and the son-in-law that we all want! How is it possible that all these characteristics dwell in just one man? Because the Lord was with him. When he was just a boy, Samuel anointed him, and "the Spirit of the Lord came upon David from that day forward" (1 Samuel 16:13). "And so it was, whenever the spirit from God was upon Saul, David would take a harp and play it with his hand. Then Saul would become refreshed and well, and the distressing spirit would depart from him" (1 Samuel 16:23). When David praised God, he "… danced before the Lord with all his might" (2 Samuel 6:14). The king had daily communion with God and enjoyed His Presence, and like a child who learns in the company of his father, he sought God daily. How could he confront the giant Goliath? Because his heart always desired Him:

> *"O God, You are my God; Early will I seek You; My soul thirsts for You; My flesh longs for You, In a dry and thirsty land Where there is no water."*
>
> Psalm 63:1

Prayer: Lord, I want to obey and serve You. Help me increase my faith. Clean my ears to hear only Your voice and my eyes to see how You see, Lord. Today, I choose to obey you in everything, Abba.

Day 37: Today I obey God in everything

"'Woman, what does your concern have to do with Me? My hour has not yet come.' His mother said to the servants, 'Whatever He says to you, do it.'"

John 2:4-5

In the middle of one of the most beautiful celebrations of the Jewish people, a wedding (union) feast, the wine (a symbol of joy and happiness) ran out. We don't know if the father of the bride got the numbers wrong, if some "tag-alongs" arrived, or they simply drank more than what was estimated, but the party was about to be over because of the lack of this precious fruit of the vine. Mary knew well whom to run to. "They have no wine" (verse 3b), she whispered in the Master's ear. Wine in the Bible represents fruitfulness and joy, healthy and full life, pleasure and holiness that only the Holy Spirit can give. That's why we see that Jesus's answer can be paraphrased like this: "What do you mean they don't have wine, woman? Am I not here? I am their true joy and My time has not yet come."

Do you also want to enjoy His wine, His life and joy, daily? Mary gives us two keys: 1) Serve ("His mother said to the servants,") and 2) Obey His Word ("Whatever He says to you, do it"). Let's look at some details that allowed those servants to enjoy a fantastic miracle: the immediate conversion of water into wine in a few simple barrels.

When Jesus told those men (who weren't His disciples) to fill six large jars with water, they "filled them up to the brim (verse 7, they obeyed the order fully, even without knowing why), and when the Master instructed them to take it to the chief servant (master of the feast), they "took it" (verse 8). Again, they obeyed immediately, without question. They didn't say, "well, if the wine has run out, the party is over, let's get paid because we're done," nor did they say, "How unfair, now we have to work more, filling up another six jars." No, despite their tiredness, the routine, and the probable inconvenience caused by yet another impertinent guest, they obeyed every instruction immediately, and then they were witnesses to a miracle that without a doubt marked their lives: the water in the jars turned into the best of wines! If we want to see miracles and be witnesses of God's power, we need to serve Him and obey Him, fully and without excuses. If Jesus is Lord in your life, love Him with all your being, serve in His Kingdom and keep His Word. Only then will He fulfill His marvelous desire to bring Heaven to Earth to dwell with you, inside of you.

> *"Jesus answered and said to him, 'If anyone loves Me, he will keep my word; and My Father will love him, and We will come to him and make Our home with him.'"*
>
> John 14:23

Prayer: Holy Spirit of God, with all my heart, I desire for my being to be turned into Your dwelling, according to Your Word. Help me obey You so that I can achieve all Your Dreams.

Day 38: I do the will of my Father

"If anyone wills to do His will, he shall know concerning the doctrine, whether it is from God or whether I speak on My own authority."

John 7:17

Jesus is close to celebrating His last Passover as a man on this earth, and there is a great division: some follow Him as the Messiah, while many others reject Him and accuse Him, even claiming that His power comes from Beelzebub, or Satan. How is it possible that people from the same town, with the same culture and such homogenous and distinct values in those days, could have completely opposing opinions about the Lord? Jesus gives us the answer in this verse: because only the one who wants to do God's will, can know (understand, receive revelation) that Jesus is sent by God. The people that don't want to do the will of God simply cannot know Him. Do you get indignant sometimes and argue with those who say that Jesus and Mary Magdalene were lovers, or that they had a son together, and even that the Master was homosexual? Or with others who think He is the same as Buddha, Sai Baba and Krishna, or who say that He wasn't Lord but rather an angel, an alien or a prophet? Are you one of those people who get immersed in long discussions, arguing in favor of the Lord, with zeal for His name? Well, the reality is that many people reject Jesus Christ today, and our insistence, discussions, and arguments are not going to change their minds. They will probably have the opposite effect, inducing them to entrench deeper into their unbelief when they see our obstinacy. Why? Because these people are not interested in knowing (understanding, receiving revelation of) God's will. That's why they demand detailed explanations for their contrived questions.

Sometimes I ask simple questions, for example: if we evolved from a monkey, why do monkeys still exist? Or if Jesus was a prophet or an angel, but not God's son, why did He say He was? Would a prophet or angel lie? And the answers I often receive are so contrived that I think it would require much more faith to believe the answer than to accept Creation or Jesus. Then I remember this verse. When a person is only personally curious, with a theoretical desire to know about God (but not really know Him) or a rather "magical" interest in God for protection or blessing, I prefer to invest my time praying for that person, alone, asking God to open their eyes:

> *"whose minds the god of this age has blinded, who do not believe, lest the light of the gospel of the glory of Christ, who is the image of God, should shine on them."*
>
> 2 Corinthians 4:4

Prayer: Holy Father, open my eyes to know You. I want to know Your will, Lord. Take the blinders of the god of this age from my eyes. I want to see how You see. Thank you, Jesus.

Day 39: Today I open up my heart

"O Corinthians! We have spoken openly to you, our heart is wide open. You are not restricted by us, but you are restricted by your own affections."

2 Corinthians 6:11-12

It's remarkable to see how difficult it is for us to show affection and compassion, even to our closest loved ones. We are so afraid to show our vulnerability that we disguise ourselves as unfeeling! Giant heavenly bodies depend on each other for their orbit, but we think we are independent. We are unable to stop our own heart for even a few seconds, but we think we are self-sufficient. How is it possible that so much knowledge makes us so ignorant? We know that one day our body will die, but we live as if it were eternal. We live "inward," focused and closed off around ourselves, like a small child who, because of immaturity, only goes after his own satisfaction, unable to sense the needs of others. But hurting others is like sticking a fingernail in your own eye, biting your own tongue, or insulting the mirror. In the same way that many people who have been abused or mistreated end up hating themselves and taking it out on themselves because of a lack of received love, human beings mistreat each other, destroying God's creation, while we think we are defending ourselves. But we have no reason to act like this, because we are very beloved. So much so that Jesus died for us.

But it's easy to see how leaves are interconnected through the branches, and the branches through the trunk, and these through the earth, the breeze, the sun and the insects. And how rivers depend on rain, oceans on rivers, and rain on oceans, and how the oceans' tides are drawn by the moon. Just like the cells in our body, we are fractions of something infinitely greater, and we urgently need to open up our hearts to understand it, embrace it, and enjoy it. To awaken to the reality that we are not individual, but interdependent entities; that we are not enemies but complements of each other; that we are not threats but help and support for each other; that we are all part of the same universe, the same creation, and that if I hurt you, I hurt the same creation of which I am a part. Let's not waste time; let's open up our hearts and souls, our humanity, to return the same to God:

> *"Now in return for the same (I speak as to children), you also be open."*
>
>   2 Corinthians 6:13

Prayer: Blessed Jesus Christ, I beg you to help me love others, to open up my heart to cover those whom it is hard for me to love with Your covering. Bless all humanity, Holy Father. Thank You, because Your hand is over all the earth.

Day 40: Today I open up my whole heart

"O Corinthians! We have spoken openly to you, our heart is wide open. You are not restricted by us, but you are restricted by your own affections."

2 Corinthians 6:11-12

When was the last time that you gave recognition to your spouse, someone on your team, or a friend, or even a stranger? When was the last time that, despite the daily racing, you noticed something beautiful? When was the last time that you paused to meditate, to be thankful, to breathe… ? And to ask for forgiveness? When was the last time that when "really important" won out over what was "less important"? How did you feel? …

Sometimes my heart reminds me of a turtle that withdraws into its shell at the slightest noise. It feels safe there, but it can't see anything. It thinks it's protected, but it's really paralyzed. It can't move. You weren't created by God to close up in a shell with internal walls that read: "known, without risk, without pain." You will probably be safe there, but at the bottom of the sea! Paul and his disciples opened up their heart to the Corinthians, but they were narrow, closed, untrusting; it was hard for them to receive and show love. Despite all the good that they received from Paul and his companions, in spite of all the power of the Gospel in action, they remained closed off, doubtful, insecure. Let's not narrow our hearts. Let's not withhold a compliment for our spouse, not ignore the blessing that our children represent, not deny help or words of refreshment to someone in battle or consolation to someone who is afflicted. This is why we are the light of the world (Matthew 5:14), to give light, to shine when darkness reigns, to keep hope alive when it has dried up for many. When a child of God comes into a place, the spiritual environment should change, the same way that dry land does with rain. Don't presume that your eyes will see or your lungs breath, because it's not by your will; rather, the will of One who is greater than you. Don't assume that time will never run out, because one day, you will certainly die. Give thanks, bless, get rid of fear, dare to be vulnerable. Only then will you grow. Open your heart to love, your mind to understand, your eyes to wake up, your mouth to bless and your hand to give. Open yourself up! Transform the world!

> *"Now in return for the same (I speak as to children), you also be open."*
>
> 2 Corinthians 6:13

Prayer: Father, I want to carry Your Holy Spirit in me in a way that wherever I go, I carry You with me. I want to be able to encourage my spouse, my children and all those I contact. I want to be an instrument of Your good and Your light, Lord Jesus.

Day 41: Today I understand Your language

"Why do you not understand My speech? Because you are not able to listen to My word."

Jesus in John 8:43

Recently, in a park close to home, I wanted to speak with a nice lady whose grandson played actively with my son Daniel, but she was only able to tell me, "I come Russia, Russia. Only Russian," and clearly, it was impossible to communicate because I don't know that language. I would have loved to be able to speak her language. She seemed like a really nice person, and the kids got along well. I could have helped her a little, and who knows? Our families could even have become friends, but if you don't know how to communicate with someone, it's difficult for a friendship to begin. If you can't share what you think or prefer, or know how that person's feelings or hopes, there isn't much to enjoy together. You can't teach her or learn from her. Something similar is happening in this verse, where Jesus explains to the religious people why they don't understand: they just don't speak His language. Despite the fact that the Master tried to explain His message of Life in the simplest way possible, using parables, stories of kings, of birds of the field and sheep, they didn't understand. Today, some people spend a long time supposedly talking with God, but their prayers show few results (like the Russian woman and me). It's because they speak to God in our earthly, natural, limited language, instead of speaking to Him in His language. It is imperative that we begin to speak God's language, that we open up and expand, and don't try to get Him to adapt to ours, which limits us and His work in our lives.

Now then, the best way to learn a new language is to study it and become friends with people who speak that language, and with God it's the same. His language can be learned by studying His Word and spending time with Him. And the more you learn, communication flows more easily and clearly, the relationship strengthens, and that friendship influences you. You don't just understand God's language, which is faith; you are filled with it. You don't just know His Word; you apply it, to yourself, your life, your marriage, and your children, understanding that that Word is Christ, and is real and always fulfilled, without exception. Then your prayers are made fresh, simple, and sincere, but above all, powerful and put to His service. Only then do you both (God and you) clearly understand what the other wants to say. Glory to the living God! Only then will you be of Him, and you will be able to hear His Word:

> *"He who is of God hears God's words; therefore you do not hear, because you are not of God."*
>
> John 8:47

Prayer: Holy Lord, open my mind and my ears to understand Your language, to see challenges as You see them, as opportunities that are always surmountable with You. I want to speak Your language because I am Yours, and you are my Papa. Thank You Lord.

Day 42: Today I only speak about my Heavenly Father

"And I know that His command is everlasting life. Therefore, whatever I speak, just as the Father has told Me, so I speak."
John 12:50

The idea of being "free" in the world implies doing whatever we want, including, if possible, acting outside of the law. That's why we toil to get money and power, to be able to do our own will without limitations. That's why we admire the rich and famous, who can do their own will (despite the fact that many of their lives are disasters). But Jesus has a different attitude: He chooses to be under the law, absolutely obedient to the Father's commandments because they produce eternal life, and He gives us the example by obeying Him in everything, even in every word that He says. He is the King of kings and Lord of lords, the greatest of every name that can be named, the fullness of God made man, and even so, the key to His success, His power, His freedom, is obedience. That's why, in Proverbs 19:16, Solomon says "He who keeps the commandment keeps his soul" Just like how every child is blessed by obeying a wise and loving father, obedience to God benefits us. God commands it for our good, not His. He doesn't need to satisfy His ego. He is humble and without complexes.

Although it seems very difficult, you and I are called to do the same. Do you want things to go well for you? Obey His commandments. Do you want freedom? Heed His instructions and statutes. Not just the Ten

Commandments from Moses, but all of His Word. For example, Paul tells us that no corrupt word should come out of our mouth, but only the one that is good and imparts grace to the hearers (Ephesians 4:29). Sometimes we speak without evaluating what we are saying, letting the words flow without a filter, murmuring about people we don't know, adding our opinion and cruel commentaries to the collective analysis about things that we don't know! In a nutshell, we are judging others with shameful freedom, but Jesus clearly said that He judges no one. Let's ask God for His Holy Spirit to remind us and even embarrass us when we fall in this trap. Eradicate the words that oppose His Word with His help. We need to live in alignment with God to be able to be free. Jesus had the knowledge to utter words of judgment and condemnation against each of us, but He didn't do it… The key, as always, is communion:

> *"For I have not spoken on My own authority; but the Father who sent Me gave Me a command, what I should say and what I should speak."*
>
> John 12:49

Prayer: Blessed Father, guide my Words. Clean my mouth so that I only pronounce messages in Your language: Faith. Help me to filter what I say through Your Holy Spirit. I don't want to speak filth, curses, bitterness or discouragement, but faith, and I want to use Your Word to bless, restore, encourage and confront others.

Day 43: Today I believe God's every Word

"But behold, you will be mute and not able to speak until the day these things take place, because you did not believe my words which will be fulfilled in their own time."

Luke 1:20

The angel did the best thing he could do with an unbeliever: mute him! Have you noticed that every time someone says, "I don't feel well," another person immediately starts launching hypotheses about the cause? "Clearly, it's this climate, the pollen, the rain, or that air conditioning…" And for pain in your bones or difficulty reading small text, there is always someone to say, "The years keep catching up with me; I'm not the same as I was before …" And so we program our mind daily for deterioration and failure. If we give something that afflicts us a cause, the next time we find ourselves in a similar situation, we will expect affliction, and it will certainly come! It's the opposite of faith: fear. That's why Job said, "… what I dreaded has happened to me" (Job 3:25b). Let the angel Gabriel mute us before we speak like that! Why?

Because these words are false. They are arguments and arrogance that raise up against knowledge of God. (2 Corinthians 10:5). They are anti-biblical, because they are against the Truth. Jesus warned, "… those things which proceed out of the mouth come from the heart, and they defile a man" (Matthew 15:18). What defiles you or cleans you, what makes you sick or heals you, what limits you or opens you up, is what you believe, and that is manifested through what you speak. That's why we should only believe and speak the Truth. Jesus Christ called the devil a "liar and the father of it [lies]" (John 8:44b), so if you and I believe him, we will be children of his lies! In fact, when we listen to his opinion about who we are, or about what we can or cannot achieve; when we doubt what God promises us in His Word, we become followers of Satan, simply because our steps follow what we believe in. Jesus continued with a shocking phrase, "But because I tell the truth, you do not believe Me" (John 8:45). We are quick to believe the lie, and slow to absorb the truth. We need to change, because only Christ's disciples "shall know the truth, and the truth shall make you free" (John 8:32). This is the difference between the believer and an unbeliever: The first hears the Word (Christ), the second the lie (the devil). If you want to reprogram yourself and be transformed to live in His Word, you should begin by making Him your Lord and master; only then will you be able to hear His Words:

> *"He who is of God hears God's words; therefore you do not hear, because you are not of God."*
>
> John 8:47

Prayer: Father, mute me if I'm going to speak what is evil and corrupt. Guard my heart from rumors and judgment so that my lips don't produce gossip. Fill my heart with Your Holy Spirit so that I only speak Your language: Faith.

Day 44: Today I understand that You are real, and I can feel You

"That which was from the beginning, which we have heard, which we have seen with our eyes, which we have looked upon, and our hands have handled, concerning the Word of life--"

1 John 1:1

I love the way John writes—how he tries to make us understand that Jesus Christ is real. He isn't a religion, a tradition, or a custom, but that He is alive and although He is the Eternal One ("from the beginning"), John and the other disciples heard Him with their ears, saw Him with their own eyes, looked upon Him and touched Him with their hands. They hugged Him, saw Him, shared with Him, listened to His voice and lived with the One Word of Life. His disciples saw Him turn water into the best wine, feed multitudes with a few loaves of bread and fish, and return sight, hearing and speech to hundreds of people who were blind, deaf and mute. They saw Him clean and smooth the skin of so many lepers; straighten the woman who was bent over, lift up paralytics, unbind Mary Magdalene and the man from Gadara in whom legion of demons lived. And above all, they were witnesses of the resurrection of the already stinky Lazarus after he had been dead for four days.

After a while walking side by side with the Master, their lives were never the same, and those common men, most of them uneducated, became the founders of the early Church that even today remains firm and keeps growing.

Did religion do this, or the relationship they had with Jesus? Only daily communion with the Messiah did it. The Lord modeled what it meant to be a son of the Most High to them, day by day, with all the duties and responsibilities, but also with the authority, rights, and benefits. None of that has changed since then. Jesus is still the same today, yesterday and forever, although we can't see Him or touch Him now. And He wants much more of you. Not just for you to respect Him and become "solemn" when you enter your church (because He isn't pleased with your perfect morals and behavior), but for your heart to be close to His. God doesn't desire your rituals in front of symbols that, according to you, represent Him. He wants you completely, your whole spirit, your soul and body, without holding anything back. That's why He created you and later bought you on the Cross. Daily, minute-by-minute, patient but passionate, He seeks your friendship and love, time alone with you. The Word of Life is desperate to have you:

> *"And you shall love the Lord your God with all your heart, with all your soul, with all your mind, and with all your strength. This is the first commandment."*
>
> Mark 12:30

Prayer: Thank You Lord for becoming more and more real in my life. Thank You because without seeing You, I perceive You, and without touching You, I feel You. I cannot touch you like John but right now I feel Your Spirit. Make me sensitive to Your Presence Lord so I know that You are closer to me than myself, in every moment.

Day 45: Today I am about Your business, Abba

"And He [12-year-old Jesus] *said to them, "Why did you seek Me? Did you not know that I must be about My Father's business?"*

Luke 2:49

That was Jesus's answer to his parents when He was still a pre-teen. This little boy had the flesh of a man, but He came from Heaven. He was there when the Earth was created and breathed the breath of life over the inert clay of Adam. He knew well that everything happens in two parallel kingdoms, interconnected through our soul; that the natural world is subject to the spiritual, and that what happens on Earth is related to what happens in Heaven. What is visible is strongly influenced by the invisible. What we sense, He knows with certainty, which is why Jesus prayed so much because He knows the Father well. You and I should pray that way. But in this passage, Jesus wasn't praying; rather, He was "… sitting in the midst of the teachers, both listening to them and asking them questions. And all who heard Him were astonished at His understanding and answers" (verses 46-47). Jesus came to announce His Kingdom to us, to model for us how to live on Earth under His Kingdom's principles. He had a mission and didn't worry about the critics, because His priority was the Father's business. And He obeyed the Father in everything.

What gets you out of bed every morning, the Father's business or just your own interests? Does your enthusiasm just depend on externalcircumstances, so that you are happy when everything goes well and unhappy when something doesn't? If He knows all your needs before you ask Him (Matthew 6:8), why not stop worrying so much about your issues and start paying more attention to the Father's Kingdom (business)? Jesus says here that it's necessary. What will you do for God today? How will you support His business? Today in your work, in every daily issue, remember that you are not there to kill time and get a monthly check; you were not created to accumulate wealth and retire at a certain age. You are here to diligently be about your Father's business. He is counting on you. Represent Him well, because after all, His business is about restoring your soul and mine, together with all of humanity. That's why He gave up His Son, who is the living example of that connection, that what you bind on Earth is bound in Heaven (Matthew 18:18). Note that despite His absolute subjection to the Father, as a parallel and as a living example of the connection between both worlds (natural and spiritual), He always obeyed Joseph and Mary.

> *"Then He went down* [12-year-old Jesus] *with them, and was subject to them, but His mother kept all these things in her heart."*
>
> Luke 2:51

Prayer: Sweet Holy Spirit, guide me today and always so all I do also works for Your Kingdom. I want to be about Your business. Help me to plant Your Word in every conversation, to have You present in every moment. I want You to be my priority and my Lord in everything. Thank You, Abba, because I know that I can always count on You.

"And no one puts new wine into old wineskins; or else the new wine bursts the wineskins, the wine is spilled, and the wineskins are ruined. But new wine must be put into new wineskins."
Mark 2:22

Holy Spirit, thank You for daily renewing my wineskin, and spilling your Holy wine over me...

Day 46: Today I am about Your business, Abba

"Then He went down [12-year-old Jesus] *with them, and was subject to them, but His mother kept all these things in her heart."*
Luke 2:51

God became man in Jesus. When His parents found Him in the temple, He was "sitting in the midst of the teachers, both listening to them and asking them questions. And all who heard Him were astonished at His understanding and answers" (verses 46-47). He wasn't rebelling against His parents, and He didn't escape maliciously to try to impress the teachers of the law. Jesus, since He was a child, simply had a priority written in the depths of His soul: to do the will of the Father. Think about this: In Jesus "dwells all the fullness of the Godhead bodily" (Colossians 2:9). He is the "Author and Finisher of our faith" (Hebrews 12:2), the "Savior of the world" (1 John 4:14), and "the Living Bread which came down from Heaven" (John 6:51), full of "grace and truth" (John 1:14). He is also the One who "upholds all things by the word of His power" (Hebrews 1:3), He is the Alpha and Omega, the beginning and the end, the King of kings and Lord of lords; however, even though He was the Lord of all and everyone, He lived on Earth, daily subject to His parents' Joseph and Mary's earthly authority.

If Jesus had been focused on Himself, He would be remembered today as a great leader, perhaps like Alexander the Great or Napoleon. But He preferred to focus on the Father, and as such, there was no rebellion to be found in His heart. Only thus could He change the history of humanity, restore the Way to the Father, and literally change the spiritual atmosphere of the Earth. In the approximately thirty-three years of life incarnate as a man on Earth, Jesus was able to defeat the self, the world, Satan on the Cross, and death, leaving the tomb empty. In the natural world, rebellion is noisy and aggressive. It attracts us because it seems to have so much power. It seems strong, but it's very weak; it gives the impression of permanence, but it's only temporary. Nothing lasting is built through rebellion. Humanity rebels against God, thinking it is independent from Him, but Jesus Christ has a different point of view. "For I have come down from heaven, not to do My own will, but the will of Him who sent Me" (John 6:38). The Master and Lord doesn't act in His own interest but according to the Father's will (interests, business). Obedience requires character, while rebellion is just a lack of it. There is a greater power in subjection than in rebellion, which is why Jesus said...

"... learn from Me, for I am gentle and lowly in heart ..."
                                                    Matthew 11:29

Prayer: Father, today I want to subject my will to Yours. Today I understand that You are God, that You are superior to, and greater than any name that can be named. I want to do Your will like You do the Father's. Guide me Jesus and give me courage and perseverance.

Day 47: Today I cry out for others

"And when they could not come near Him because of the crowd, they uncovered the roof where He was. So when they had broken through, they let down the bed on which the paralytic was lying."

Mark 2:4

Jesus was preaching in His own house in Capernaum, and "many gathered together, so that there was no longer room to receive them, not even near the door" (verse 2). Four men who came carrying a paralytic man and weren't able to reach Him didn't give up upon seeing the multitude. Instead, they came up with a more drastic method: climb to the top of Jesus's house, open a big hole in the roof, and lower the sick man through it, giving a beautiful lesson in what strong intercession for those in need really means. They opened the heavens (the roof) to put their sick friend in contact with the One in whom the Fullness of the Godhead dwells (Colossians 2:9). His answer didn't make them wait: "When Jesus saw their faith, He said to the paralytic, 'Son, your sins are forgiven.'" The Lord had accepted their intercession and heard their petition; the paralytic was forgiven and healed at once, thanks to the faith of those who brought him (although they destroyed the Master's house).

If you want to really know the power of God, I invite you to start praying for others, interceding for those who don't know or seek Him. Cry out for those many who believe they don't need Him and even for those who call themselves atheists (literally: without God). Don't argue with them because they don't know their own ignorance. It's difficult to live without hope! There is so much need for God, and many who don't even realize it! Pray for those who criticize, judge and curse you (Matthew 5:44), and if you want to increase your intimacy with Him, don't tell anyone. Let it be a secret between you and Papa. That will protect you from all forms of spiritual pride. You need to persevere, to persist without falling away, until you open the Heavens, until you see God's goodness manifest itself, but you shouldn't do it in your own strength. Rather, do it in the strength of the one God. Our work consists of lifting up that person's need to the One who can do everything, and persisting until He gives us an answer. God will listen to you and will delight in you. Perhaps He will test your perseverance and love for others. Sometimes He will give you a burden for them in your heart. The world needs more intercessors, because those who have a rightly available heart are few. He needs you:

> *"So I sought for a man among them who would make a wall, and stand in the gap before Me on behalf of the land, that I should not destroy it; but I found no one."*
>
> Ezekiel 22:30

Prayer: Holy Father, teach me to intercede for others, for so many who are in such difficult conditions. Let my heart look like Yours, Jesus. Put compassion for souls in my soul, because they are Yours, and they are lost. Give me a humble, compassionate and interceding heart. Thank You Father, because You receive me in Your army against darkness.

Day 48: Today I call out to God for His children

"… and he will answer from within and say, 'Do not trouble me; the door is now shut, and my children are with me in bed; I cannot rise and give to you?'"

Luke 11:7

I heard the most beautiful explanation of this parable from Apostle Guillermo Maldonado: A man went to knock on his friend's door at midnight to ask him for bread for another friend who just got in from traveling, because he didn't have anything "to set before him" (verse 5-6). The central character is the intercessor (you and me), who knocks on the friend's (Jesus) door at midnight to ask for bread for another friend (the person in need), because he (the intercessor) doesn't have any food to offer him. The intercessor asks for three loaves (verse 5): the Father, the Son, and the Holy Spirit. We are called to cry out to God for others because the Lord promises to answer us. "I say to you, though he will not rise and give to him because he is his friend, yet because of his persistence he will rise and give him as many as he needs" (verse 8). It's not an accident that Jesus told this beautiful parable just after teaching His disciples (and us) to pray the model that we know as the Lord's Prayer.

It is interesting that in the first verse, Jesus pretends to be occupied with his own issues and uninterested in ours ("Do not trouble me; the door is now shut"), which challenges us to insist, to badger Him (at midnight), to persevere. Sometimes He tests us with obstacles so that He can measure how far our faith can carry us, like those four who brought a paralytic man to Jesus through the roof of the Master's house. You and I cannot heal or free others in our own power, much less convince them with discussions and arguments, because only God can give us the true bread (John 6:32-35), but we should cry out for those whose souls are malnourished, heavy, worn out, withered. In addition to this, interceding is a powerful way to increase your communion with God, "knocking" on your friend Jesus's door, to ask Him for His mercy for other people, whether they are your family, friends and acquaintances, public figures or those in imminence (authorities), regions and entire nations, and of course, your enemies. Start right now. It will get His attention, because those who pray and call out His name daily are few:

> *"And there is no one who calls on Your name, who stirs himself up to take hold of You, for You have hidden Your face from us, and have consumed us because of our iniquities."*
>
> Isaiah 64:7

Prayer: Lord Jesus, give me Your precious Bread of Life, and guide me to give it out like You did with the apostles. I want those who eat of Your Word to multiply. Open my mind and heart to the needs of humanity, and make me a channel for Your blessing to flow through to them.

Day 49: I am wheat

"But when the grain had sprouted and produced a crop, then the tares also appeared."

Matthew 13:26

The weed darnel [tares] is so similar to wheat that in some places it is called "false wheat." Later, in verse 38, Jesus explains that the "good seeds" (from which wheat grows) "are the sons of the kingdom, but the tares are the sons of the wicked one," thus the sons of the kingdom and of the devil look the same at first glance. That's why the disciples had no idea who would betray the Lord, and Pilate was confident that the people would choose Jesus. How is it possible that the sons of the enemy are confused with the sons of the kingdom (being so different on the inside), and why can't we detect the tares to protect ourselves from their malice? How can we grow tied together as if we were from the same family? Well, Jesus clearly differentiates: the wheat bears fruit; the tares don't…

Now, the question is: which one are we? Are we sure that we are wheat, or it is possible that we are confused tares? How do we know for sure? Living among wheat and tares, could we not eventually get confused? Solomon warns, "Every way of man is right in his own eyes, but the Lord weighs the hearts" (Proverbs 21:2), so our indulgence doesn't mean anything. What matters is what is really in our heart. That's why we should take a look at ourselves, because we could be part of the problem. Even the anointed king David cried out to God, saying, "Cleanse me from secret faults," (Psalm 19:12) because the fact that we judge this or that to be appropriate or not, according to our own culture, education, preferences, or customs, doesn't mean anything, because we simply are not the judges. The Father is the One who will judge, so ask yourself, and ask Him, what is in your heart: wheat or tares? For example, what do you plant every day, every time you speak? Some take a lot of pleasure in gossip and think it's tolerable because many people do it, but that isn't so (Matthew 5:2). Others think that adultery or fornication are natural and can't be avoided, and that one little sin here and there won't take you to hell. Better not to run the risk and to sincerely ask ourselves: what is my fruit? That will be His measurement...

> *"You will know them by their fruits. Do men gather grapes from thorn bushes or figs from thistles? Even so, every good tree bears good fruit, but a bad tree bears bad fruit."*
>
> Matthew 7:16-17

Prayer: Father, I beg you to forgive me for the many times in which you hoped that I was wheat, but I turned out to be tares. Forgive me for every conflict that I have created, every judgment I have passed, and every dissention that I have caused. Clean me to bear fruit in You. Thank You, Lord, for Your mercy.

Day 50: I am His fruit

He shall see the labor of His soul, and be satisfied..."

Isaiah 53:11

After describing the many sufferings that Jesus would encounter centuries later in detail (verses 3-11), the prophet takes an unexpected turn. He stops talking about the torments the Lord would go through and moves on to explain the ultimate reason for all that sacrifice (you, me and all of humanity), and then he tells us the finale: "He [Jesus] shall...be satisfied." Let's try to grasp the depth of this: we believe that we lack courage, but we are the prize for which He bet everything. We feel useless, but He couldn't stand living without us, which is why He risked it all. Sometimes we feel like we are only thorns and thistles, but He calls us and considers us His fruit; we imagine Him to be solemn and distant, but He calls us brothers (John 10:17). We feel like earthly sinners, but He calls us friends (John 15:14); we come to Him ashamed, but He receives us satisfied, and with joy in His heart. Jesus isn't just a martyr. He is the greatest of all heroes, and he doesn't love you for your success or merits, but for what you are: His greatest creation! Do you only love your children when they get good grades? No? Neither does God! Did Jesus wait to find out how you and I would behave to decide whether or not to go to that torment on the Cross? No! He gave Himself up long before we were born.

Let's get rid of all false identity, because He gave us a new and unique one: His. And He made us worthy. Solomon says it another way: "Go, eat your bread with joy, and drink your wine with a merry heart; for God has already accepted your works" (Ecclesiastes 9:7). Jesus Christ made us coheirs by His grace (Romans 8:17). Not only did He create us but later, after we abandoned Him, He also bought us, justified us, paid all our debts and returned our identity, our intrinsic real value to us. You are a special treasure to God (Exodus 19:5). Don't let anyone trick you or damage your self-esteem! Don't ever let anyone distort your self-image again! You are a child of the Most High. Anytime a child is nice to my children, I automatically like them. We are like God in this, because John says, "he who acknowledges the Son has the Father also" (1 John 2:23). Well, just like that, when you receive Christ, do you know what happens? The Father sees you the same as Jesus! Draw near to Him, receive Him in your soul, be the fruit of His affliction and make Him satisfied, because:

"Likewise, I say to you, there is joy in the presence of the angels of God over one Sinner who repents."

Luke 15:10

Prayer: Thank You Lord for adopting me under Your covering. Thank You because Your sacrifice on the Cross of Calvary restored the bridge that separated me from Your Grace. Thank You because I am part of the fruit of Your affliction. Help me to live my life according to Your principles so that You are satisfied. I am Your beloved child, in whom You are well pleased.

Day 51: Today I give place to Jesus in everything

"'Be angry, and do not sin.' Do not let the sun go down on your wrath, nor give place to the devil."

Ephesians 4:26-27

What would you do if, at the moment you sat down to watch a movie with your whole family, your spouse said, "Don't sit there; that seat is reserved for the Devil?" Would you leave a seat open at the table at dinnertime, maybe a space in the backseat of your car or in that old rocking chair beside your bed, so Satan could sit in it? I suppose you wouldn't, at least voluntarily, but according to this quote, if you let anger remain in you, you will sin, and you are giving "place to the devil." You will be opening a door, a channel, an access, so he can enter into your life, and through that path, into the lives of others.

We live in a tense world, full of pressures and injustices that stress us out, and it's not always easy to maintain control. Anyone can get angry, and as someone once said, "we all have the right to a bad day." We can have a bad moment because of something disagreeable, and be uncomfortable; feeling rage or frustration is completely normal. However, we shouldn't stay in that state. We need to shake off that annoyance, that disturbance, or otherwise we will make a mistake (sin) and lose our communion with God. I know believers who falsely fear even mentioning the name of the Devil or Satan, and use the term "the enemy" (only if strictly necessary) to keep from naming him directly, ignoring what Jesus said about us: "Behold, I give you the authority to trample on serpents and scorpions, and over all the power of the enemy, and nothing shall by any means hurt you" (Luke 10:19). However, some of these people have a hard time ignoring a little mistreatment, a brusque answer or a minor injustice. They feel afraid to even mention Satan, but without knowing it, they give him a seat in their houses through inability to ignore a fault, a small mistreatment or a minor inattention. How is that possible? We should learn to look over offenses, to ignore gossip and murmuring, to bless those who curse us but do good to those who hate us. We shouldn't judge so that we won't be judged (Matthew 7:1), and we should forgive all offenses so that our Father in Heaven will forgive all of ours (Matthew 6:12, 14-15). Don't give the devil a place; instead, give place to the Word of God. Let that seat in your soul be only for Jesus, and He will live in you:

> *"Jesus answered and said to him, 'If anyone loves Me, he will keep my word; and My Father will love him, and We will come to him and make Our home with him.'"*
>
> John 14:23

Prayer: Holy Spirit, help me to undo all my anger. Help me to be more patient and humble, and to not create big problems out of little things. Thank You, because I can get angry, but because I also can always reflect, and like a child, return quickly to communion with You and Your peace. Thank You, Lord, because you work lovingly on my character.

Day 52: Today I am aware:
I listen and I see

"Because, although they knew God, they did not glorify Him as God, nor were thankful, but became futile in their thoughts, and their foolish hearts were darkened. Professing to be wise, they became fools,"
Romans 1:21-22

Many people call themselves atheists, because, in their opinion, there isn't palpable evidence that God exists, but the word atheist simply means "without God." They think they are denying Him, but what happens is that they don't have Him. It's like someone who has never fallen in love asserting that love doesn't exist so she calls herself "un-lovable." But if someone tells you that music doesn't exist, would you look for an explanation in the violin or the guitar, or in the ears of the one who makes that assertion? Surely you would think that person is deaf because you have heard wonderful music many times. Paul declares that the evidence that God is real is before us, "For since the creation of the world His invisible attributes are clearly seen, being understood by the things that are made, even His eternal power and Godhead, so that they are without excuse," (verse 20). Jesus, on His part, seems to warn that many will not hear: "He who has ears to hear, let him hear" (Matthew 11:15, 13:19), which is why it is possible that some "seeing, they may see and not perceive, and hearing they may hear and not understand…" (Mark 4:12).

The Bible expresses a secret out loud: God "… regards the lowly; but the proud He knows from afar" (Psalm 138:6). The Holy Spirit is only attracted to places where He is believed and honored. If someone disregards Him, He doesn't draw near, and that person, upon not being able to perceive Him, believes they have confirmation of their hypothesis: God cannot exist. It's like mistreating everyone and asserting, "Love doesn't exist, because nobody loves me." Our nature tends to evaluate and judge the unknown based on what we know. That is why the Pharisees didn't notice the Messiah. They were waiting for a powerful king galloping in according to their paradigms, not a humble carpenter riding a donkey. Like the little frog that, in its little pond decides to deny the existence of the ocean or the fish that thinks the external world is a vision in the glass of the fish bowl, those who deny God trick themselves, and "professing to be wise, they become fools." The invisible God reveals Himself through the marvelous visible, but only the attentive eyes of the children perceive it:

> "...To you it has been given to know the mystery of the kingdom of God; but to those who are outside, all things come in parables, so that 'Seeing they may see and not perceive, and hearing they may hear and not understand; lest they should turn, and their sins be forgiven them.'"
>
> Mark 4:11-12

Prayer: Thank You, Jesus, for allowing me to know the mystery of Your Salvation. I beg you to never let my heart be futile, so that You, the High and Lifted Up, will never abandon my body and I will always be Your temple. I cry out for those who live without You, Lord. I ask you to have mercy and open their eyes. Thank You, Papa!

Day 53: Today I see clearly

"Nevertheless when one turns to the Lord, the veil is taken away."
2 Corinthians 3:16

In the year 1996 I had a successful operation for increasing nearsightedness that forced me to wear glasses. I remember that the day after surgery, when the plastic covers were removed, the doctor's office looked very different, bright, and the objects were clear, well defined. Only then did I sense how distorted my vision had been. Something similar can happen when you have an invisible veil covering your spiritual eyes, because you don't sense what you have, and just like a fish in a fishbowl, you can't envision the ocean. What he sees through the glass tells him that there is something out there but, as he can't understand it or swim to it, he assumes it isn't real. Our mind perceives the spiritual world and is capable of great things, but it can also be veiled, centered only on what is visible and touchable, and frequently, can guide us to perceive a portion as the whole. For this reason, Paul speaks of those "whose minds the god of this age [Satan] has blinded, who do not believe" (2 Corinthians 4:4); therefore, it is feasible that something spiritual blocks our minds, as Jesus has already warned: "so that seeing they may see and not perceive, and hearing they may hear and not understand; lest they should turn, and their sins be forgiven them" (Mark 4:12). When Jesus gave up His Spirit on the Cross of Calvary, "The veil of the temple was torn in two from top to bottom" (Matthew 27:51). This veil hid the most holy place, the place where the Presence of God physically dwelled. It was only accessible for the high priest, only once a year, and only to ask forgiveness for the people (Hebrews 9:7). But its rupture, starting at Jesus's sacrifice, represents reconciliation between God and humans, between created humanity and its Creator. The separation that our illusion of independence has caused between God and us was rent, dissolved, destroyed. It no longer exists, and the Cross of Calvary is the bridge that unites us, brings us together, and reconciles us with our Creator. All the barriers created by our sins and rebellion were pulverized and destroyed. Jesus Christ defeated darkness and erased all of our debts and mistakes, our illnesses and curses, our lack and limitations. Now we have direct access to the Father, not just to ask forgiveness, but also to have communion, relation, and friendship:

> *"Let us therefore come **boldly to the throne of grace**, that we may obtain mercy and find grace to help in time of need."*
>
> Hebrews 4:16

Prayer: Blessed Father, thank You for sending Jesus Christ to rend the veil. Thank You, because Your Word is a lamp to my feet and wash for my eyes. I always want to walk in Your truth, in Your holiness, in Your power. Thank You, because being Your child, I can confidently approach the throne of Your Grace and find Your mercy to help me, always.

Day 54: Today I thank the Lord

"So when Jesus had received the sour wine, He said, 'It is finished!'
And bowing His head, He gave up His spirit."

John 19:30

The last words spoken by Christ on the Cross were a cry of victory: "It is finished!" The Lord had done it, He had defeated Satan forever, and His mission was finished, accomplished, complete; absolutely nothing left to do. The divine plan doesn't consider that we get sick to die but that once we finish what God created us for, we return home. Jesus paid for our sins and carried our sicknesses (Isaiah 53:5-6), He carried our curses (Galatians 3:13) and our poverty (2 Corinthians 8:9); so that if you, right now, "…confess with your mouth the Lord Jesus and believe in your heart that God raised Him from the dead, you will be saved" (Romans 10:9). What are these verses telling us? That by believing in Jesus Christ and His redeeming work, we are redeemed, forgiven, freed from debt. We enter into coverage under His covenant and we have access to the throne of His grace (Hebrews 4:16). We don't have to make any sacrifice! He already did it all! It is finished!

Many people believe they should sacrifice and pay the price that Jesus already paid. That is why they invented Purgatory, a place of torment and punishment where someone who believes in God but failed morally suffers for an undetermined period of time until his sins are expiated. However, the Bible doesn't mention this doctrine for a simple reason: it is anti-Christian. If you, having believed in God and having sincerely repented before Him, have to pay a price, then Jesus's sacrifice wasn't enough, nor His grace. Although people who flagellate themselves, carry heavy images on certain holidays or martyr themselves by traveling long distances on their knees, damaging their body which is the temple of the Holy Spirit (1 Corinthians 6:19) seek to honor God, they are degrading Him and have the vanity to assume that our Lord Jesus Christ's sacrifice wasn't enough, which is why they need to finish (consummate) what Jesus started. But He did finish the only possible sacrifice for our salvation, purchasing us with the price of His precious life, which is why He made it very clear that there is no other:

> *"I am the way, the truth, and the life. No one comes to the Father except through Me."*
>
> John 14:6

Prayer: Thank You Jesus because on that Cross, you defeated the enemy that oppressed us, and now we have freedom through Your Blood. Thank You because you finished Your work and sacrifice, and so redeemed us. Free me from all religious mentalities that try to make me holier than what You have made me, and try to get more dignity than what You have granted me.

Day 55: Today I am free from condemnation

"There is therefore now no condemnation to those who are in Christ Jesus, who do not walk according to the flesh, but according to the Spirit."

Romans 8:1

I try to imagine what a repentant criminal would feel like upon hearing the judge pronounce his verdict: Not guilty! Those simple words mean that he has been given a new opportunity; that he will not suffer prison, with its abuse, loneliness, and violence. Now he can be with his loved ones and have control of his own time. If he wants, he can feel the rays of the sun and the drops of water from walking in the rain. He is free—no more oppression or torment. Now he has another opportunity, because no condemnation weighs on his shoulders. I suppose that the sick person who reads the words "total remission" on his medical exam results, and to a lesser extent, someone who reads a stamp saying "paid" on his mortgage documents could feel something similar.

So now, you and I were children of disobedience (Ephesians 2:2) and fell short of the glory of God (Romans 3:23). How do you feel to know that, two thousand years ago, the Judge of judges declared the verdict "not guilty" over your name? And when all your mistakes and malice were presented to Him, He said, "paid on the Cross;" and even before the pain of illness came to you, Jesus said, "healed by my wounds;" and when the lawsuit is opened against you detailing all your iniquities (as well as those of your parents and grandparents), He said, "redeemed on the Cross." When Jesus says "healed," it means completely healed, and when the Bible says, "there is no condemnation," it is because not even a trace of it exists. Don't accuse yourself anymore; don't blame yourself; don't keep lamenting for what you could have done better this morning or thirty years ago. Invite Christ to enter into your heart and return to the path you were created for. Return to His original plan of blessing and happiness for you and your loved ones, and then you will be able to rise up and confidently declare, "There is no condemnation for me!" I invite you to do it now. Declare out loud, "There is no condemnation for me!" Repeat it; let this truth penetrate the strongholds of your mind and permeate you soul. Allow His Spirit to guide you so that you will live according to Him. Hear His Word, believe in the One who sent Him, and there will be no condemnation for you, because you will have passed from death into life.

> *"Most assuredly, I say to you, he who hears My word and believes in Him who sent Me has everlasting life, and shall not come into judgment, but has passed from death into life."*
> John 5:24

Prayer: A billion thanks Jesus Christ because I am free from all condemnation. Despite my weakness, my lowness, and my mistakes, You believed and believe in me. That is why I am free from all condemnation. I am found innocent by Your Grace. Thank You for erasing my evil and nailing all my sin on that heavy Cross. Thank You, my precious Redeemer.

Day 56: Today I cling only to You

"Whom have I in heaven but You? And there is none upon earth that I desire besides You.

Psalm 73:25

All throughout the Scriptures we are shown the complete interconnection between the spiritual and the natural. David lives on earth but has God in Heaven, and the fact of having Him in the spiritual satisfies him so much that "there is none upon earth that I desire besides You." The spiritual prevails over the natural. When you are full of God, the desire for earthly things bothers you less, but it's not about choosing poverty. David really possessed very abundant riches but, different than what happens with most of us, those riches didn't possess him. He enjoyed to the max all the many benefits that he received, sharing and sacrificing generously for God and others, being fully and daily aware of Who provided it (Psalm 16:1a). That is why he doesn't cling to riches or to the prestige or power that they can give him, but he clings to the One who provides. The good in David's life comes from his intimate relationship with God, and the economic wellbeing was only one of the many good consequences of deeply loving a generous Father, of daily living with Him…

I personally love to watch water run, not stagnant; to hear the birds in the trees, not cages; to enjoy time, not try to trap it. God blesses you with life and wellbeing so you can enjoy it and bless others, not so that you cling to His gifts. On a cloudy day we look for the sun, we don't try to trap a little ray of light while it happens, because it goes so fast… but the Sun remains. The greatest of all blessings that God wants to give you is Himself. Nothing greater than He who contains all and loves you so much that He gave up His life to have you "in Heaven and on earth," in the spiritual and the material. He wants to give you more, much more. His Grace has many forms and His goodness flows abundantly and constantly over those who sincerely desire Him and honor Him. The question is: do you love God or only pursue His gifts? We frequently, desperately pursue the earthly (accumulating objects, jewels and toys) because it validates us externally but, after all, nothing belongs to us. It is all on loan. Jesus Christ paid the price of all your debts, not missing one, with all His blood. How can you possess something if you yourself are not yours? Enjoy God's blessings without clinging. Cling to God!

"My soul follows close behind You; Your right hand upholds me."
Psalm 63:8

Prayer: Father, I understand that knowing You is the greatest of Your blessings. Today I want to focus more on Your Kingdom and less on everything else because the one who follows You lacks nothing. Thank You Father because my efforts for Your Kingdom are not in vain. Guide me and use me!

Day 57: Today I have intimacy with my Father

"Because 'All flesh is as grass, and all the glory of man as the flower of the grass. The grass withers, and its flower falls away,'"
1 Peter 1:24

Grass is tenacious like the human will. It clings to life, and as long as it has a little humidity, it survives. It withstands the sun and rain, the heat of the day and the cold of night, and it adapts to different seasons and terrains, at many different angles. But without water…it dries up irremediably. I think the grass's secret is that although it's exposed, it clings to the covered part; although it is visible, it connects to the invisible, and its hidden root anchors it to the earth, seeking to bind to its texture, germinating and extending its tendrils little by little, without anyone noticing. Because rain dries rapidly on the outside but inside, underground, the water stays like a subterranean river. Although you see it fall and splash outside, it is below, inside, in the hidden, where it really collects… The flower, for its side, is different. It is fragile, because its focus is on the external, not on the secret; in the visible and not the intimate. Grass can live without flowers but a flower cannot live without grass. It depends on the grass that, extracting life from under the earth, nurtures it and gives it the freshness that makes it beautiful.

You and I are like the grass, because although we are visible, our life comes from the hidden, from something intimate that connects to our root, and we are much more than what the mirror reflects. Although we are covered in flesh and blood runs through our veins, we are spirits; although we come from dust, God breathed His breath of life into us (Genesis 2:7). Without the Water of the Spirit, we dry up. Only by drinking from it daily we do produce flowers, like crowns, and fruit. But the focus shouldn't be on the flower, but on the root, on the source where the water is. Do you want to bloom and bear good fruit? Focus less on the external (the flower and the fruit), and cultivate the root. If your attention is always on the flower or the fruit you produce, you will dry up, because though the dew refreshes the petals, it doesn't nurture us, and with the sun, it withers. The flower is a consequence, not a cause; it is beautiful but it doesn't create, it doesn't reproduce. Let's learn from the grass and seek the subterranean river of Living Water. We will only remain when we are planted by His spring. No one counts withered flowers; rather, they look for new ones. Don't live from your glory but from the Holy Spirit. Be concerned with Him, the root, and the Father will fill you with flowers:

> "But you, when you go pray, go into your room, and when you have shut your door, pray to your Father who is in the secret place; and your Father who sees in secret will reward you openly."
>
> Matthew 6:6

Prayer: Blessed God, I want to have continual intimacy with you in the secret place. You are my sustenance and the root of all good. You have eternal Life so I ask for Your living water to always flow in me. Thank You Lord because You nourish much more than my body.

Day 58: God guides my steps

"Because he has set his love upon Me, therefore I will deliver him; I will set him on high, because he has known My name."

Psalm 91:14

God manifests two desires of His heart here: 1) to free us and 2) to set us on high, and so He establishes the necessary condition to achieve each goal. First, we should put our love in Him. Did you know that you decide where you put your love? Jesus says, "For where your treasure is, there your heart will be also" (Matthew 6:21), so your feelings and attention gravitate toward what you value and love. If you think about the relationships that you treasure (like your family or your best friend, for example), you probably maintain frequent contact with them, sharing intimacy and advice because you each have a certain influence in the other's life, and appreciate each other's opinion. It isn't very different with the Holy Spirit. Does what God think about you according to His Word matter to you? Do you take time to be alone with Him? Do you call on Him frequently to know how He is and what He wants to do in you and through you in the world? If your answer is yes, then you have put your love in Him…

The second condition is to know His name. One thing is to believe that God exists somewhere and another, very different, to know Him personally. Not only knowing that He is real but He is also alive and cares about you. The word translated as "to know" in the Bible indicates a much closer communion than knowing someone's phone number: "Now Adam knew Eve his wife, and she conceived…" (Genesis 4:1). It is intimate knowledge. You didn't get to know your spouse by repeating prayers or visualizing her without sharing time together, opening your heart and caring for hers. That is why you came up with ways to be alone together, to talk, touch and kiss. Well, you get to know God similarly: sharing time with Him, knowing Him as Father, and discovering yourself as His child, experiencing His Presence. The "name," on the other hand, refers to reputation, to fame. It's one thing to believe that God can do miracles and another to know His power because you have experienced it. It's one thing to think God is good, and another to know, in the deepest part of your being, that He loves you deeply, that you are His special treasure (Exodus 19:5) and that His plans are always for good and peace for you (Jeremiah 29:11). Jesus loves you so much that He gave Himself up for you. He wants to free you and set you on high, to heal you and make you prosper in everything:

> *"Beloved, I pray that you may prosper in all things and be in health, just as your soul prospers."*
>
> 3 John 1:2

Prayer: Holy Father, guide my steps every day. I want to spend more time with You, know You more, live under Your shade forever. Thank You for liking my company. I love You Jesus.

Day 59: Today He strengthens me

"…that He would grant you, according to the riches of His glory, to be strengthened with might through His Spirit in the inner man,"

Ephesians 3:16

When we think about a treasure that comes from God, perhaps we imagine a chest full of jewels, an easy task to complete (that demands little effort and time) or a "perfect" loving relationship, without any discord but with absolute and always spontaneous compatibility. But if you think about it well, any of these things would weaken you. A life that is too easy is comfortable, but it atrophies. Where there is no wind, trees are weak, and in the places where winter is intense, they build better houses. It's obvious that the leopard didn't develop so much strength by pacing in the grass, and something that athletes know well is that you can't get stronger if you don't push harder. No one runs faster or jumps higher if it doesn't sweat for every millisecond, every centimeter gained…

Something similar happens with the Spirit. One of the treasures that God wants to give you according to His riches in glory is inner strength. The apostle isn't talking about physical strength or mental power. Neither is He saying that we need to try to be perfect. What He wants is your soul; all of it, complete, only for Him. He wants you to bloom and bear fruit, but not by working on the branches but the root, inside, in the intimate parts, and sometimes, in the dark places…

When you invite Him to enter into your life, although you seem to be the same on the outside, He begins to transform you, and you become a "new creation" (2 Corinthians 5:17). He won't put makeup on your face; He will clean up your heart. He won't cover you with eccentric clothing, but He will hold up a mirror to your naked soul. This inner strength is the spiritual power that is born inside of you and guides you to invite the All Powerful to reign in your life, to fill your character, to inundate your emotions and your mind. Paul refers to maintaining a persistent faith, a faith that is strong, focused like a laser beam on His Word and not distracted by the fears of this world. You can have joy in the midst of challenges because you know that what you are living through is temporary, and that victory is already yours, because Christ conquered it for you two thousand years ago, on the Cross. Move from the comfort zone to the growth zone. Jesus wants to strengthen you so that you reach greater victories. He is a God of challenges, advances and achievements, and for that He needs to train you so you can do it. Only when you are strengthened in Him will He place the precious oil of His anointing on you. Only when your inner being belongs to Him, He will strengthen it.

> *"He gives power to the weak, and to those who have no might He increases strength."*
>
> Isaiah 40:29

Prayer: Strengthen me Lord Jesus. Strengthen my faith, my conviction of the truth and the supernatural nature of Your Word. Help me to be persistent in seeking Your Kingdom. I want to be diligent in serving You and humanity, in the name of Jesus.

Day 60: Today I pursue my dreams and set aside distractions

"But when the grain had sprouted and produced a crop, then the tares also appeared."

Matthew 13:26

The tares only appeared after the grain sprouted, when the good seed bore fruit. I believe that is a spiritual law. Once you start bearing fruit, weeds [tares] appear, and you know where? Very close to you, like in the wheat, unperceived but right at your side. It generally comes like a discreet form of envy that someone has and manifests itself as constant criticism of your achievements and the tendency to minimize everything you do. Other times someone wants to direct your eyes toward what you don't have instead of what you do have, trying to plant seeds of greed in your soul, to make the happiness and thankfulness flee from your heart. Occasionally it disguises itself as "wise and realistic" advice of that friend who warns you that you "need to act," that you can't sit and wait on God. The job of the weed is simple: to convince you that you are not special. It will tell you that bearing fruit isn't the primary goal, that you and she are exactly the same…

But God has a different opinion. Even Pilate "knew that the chief priests had handed Him [Jesus] over because of envy" (Mark 15:10). Those who sought the Messiah so hard couldn't see Him, even when they had Him right in front of them. The priests without fruit (tares or weeds) couldn't stand the Wheat (John 12:24). The same will happen with you, if you are wheat. Make sure to move constantly and daily toward your destination. Follow your dreams; persevere and bear fruit. Don't let any weeds detain you or distract you! Now, if no one is judging or criticizing you; if there is no opposition in your life and no one envies you, if you don't perceive the roots of weeds trying to wrap around your roots, consider your ways. You probably aren't moving toward what God has for you. Re-check yourself, take time and evaluate yourself, make sure that you are not that weed. Don't give up because things seem to go well for evil people. Don't let their appearance confuse you, because their destination is not good. God hasn't yet pulled the weeds, just to protect the wheat. When the men told the owner (God) about the wheat: "'Do you want us then to go and gather them up?' He said, 'No, lest while you gather up the tares you also uproot the wheat with them.'" (Matthew 13:28b-29) The Father's answer is as full of mercy as Divine justice:

> *"Let both grow together until the harvest, and at the time of harvest I will say to the reapers, 'First gather together the tares and bind them in bundles to burn them, but gather the wheat into my barn.'"*
>
> Matthew 13:30

Prayer: Today I get rid of all weeds that seek to asphyxiate my dreams. Today I close my ears to the enemy's words spoken by those who surround me. I close off to all words of discouragement, impossibility and fear. What You want to do is already written, who will hinder it? I trust that all is possible for the one who believes in You, Lord. Thank You!

**"Father, I desire that they also whom
You gave Me may be with Me where I am..."**
John 17:24a

*Lord, one by one, demolish the paradigms that make
my soul believe that You and I are separated.*

Day 61: Today I believe God for new and greater things

"And Zacharias said to the angel, 'How shall I know this? For I am an old man, and my wife is well advanced in years.'"

Luke 1:18

The angel Gabriel brought marvelous news to Zachariah: despite Elisabeth, his wife's infertility, and both of their advanced ages (verse 7), she would give birth to a son that would have a new and different name: John (not Zachariah II or Zachariah Junior). Additionally, the powerful Angel told him, "he will be great in the sight of the Lord," (verse 15) and if that weren't enough, that he would be assigned a great mission: That child John, when he grew up, "will turn many of the children of Israel to the Lord their God" (verse 16). Zacharias was a spiritual leader; he and his wife "walked in all the commandments and ordinances of the Lord blameless" (verse 16). That is why he was ministering in the temple that day, and as if that weren't enough, he was seeing the glory of the angel Gabriel in his full splendor, before his very eyes. However, his question was unexpected, I think even for Gabriel: "How shall I know this? For I am an old man, and my wife is well advanced in years" (verse 18). In other words: "Thanks for the message angel, but how it is possible for something like that to happen? It's not possible or logical. It doesn't make sense... We are old and barren; I think it's too late, Lord." Two opposing forces collided: on one side, God's Word, true and irrefutable, and on the other, Zachariah's mind, which was (like yours and mine, many times) too narrow to imagine the Truth.

What type of truth fits in your mind today? Is it saturated with custom and what has always been done, or you have room to believe in greater things? Sometimes without our notice, we limit the Truth so it will fit in our mind (that's how religion is born) instead of opening our faith to embrace that Truth. But could we minimize a train so it can pass through a tunnel in a children's park? No, you would have to tear down the park and build better rails. The great collision between the Truth and our faith should pulverize our strongholds and paradigms instead of trying to minimize God. We should open up our possibilities with God instead of limiting Him, playing like we ourselves are gods. Do you know what the angel did when he heard Zachariah denying the truth? He protected him and others from his unbelieving words. How? Leaving him mute:

> *"But behold, you will be mute and not able to speak until the day these things take place, because you did not believe my words which will be fulfilled in their own time."*
>
> Luke 1:20

Prayer: Lord, help me to be flexible. Renew my mind so that Your Word finds space in it and can enter. Help me to understand that formulas and paradigms don't work with You. You are creative and supernatural, and your Grace has many forms so destroy all religious rigidity in me and all loftiness that rises up against Your knowledge. Thank You for renewing me, Lord.

Day 62: Today I welcome challenges

"In the day when I cried out, you answered me, and made me bold with strength in my soul."

Psalm 138:3

I once heard of an indigenous tribe who, when a woman gave birth to twins, she was punished as an adulterer because they believed that each baby came from a different father. I imagine that even each pregnant woman believed it as well, until it happened to her. Just like us, they had an intense need to connect the effects with their causes to feel in control. How many times we do narrate all of the weather-related reasons in detail (heat, rain, air conditioning) that causes us a simple cold? We need to connect the consequence with the cause to try to understand the world and anticipate what's coming, so we don't suffer the same. In that way, we manage to decrease (or at least we think we do) as much as possible the psychological impact of one of our greatest enemies: uncertainty.

But what if that circumstance that you face doesn't come from a cause in your past but from an opportunity in your future? What if that trial that seems so threatening only happened to develop our character so we could fulfill our destiny? All throughout the Bible, we see how men and women who God used with power faced challenges that weren't punishments for their errors; on the contrary; they were trampolines to develop their potential to the max. David faces great trials (like Goliath for example), achieving fame, riches, and influence, and here we can see one of the causes of his great achievements: when he cried out to God for help, God didn't get him out of the problem. He "made me [David] bold with strength in my soul." Why? So that he could go further. Where does a warrior develop? In battle! And the athlete? On the court, in the gym, making continued efforts. Moses was made humble for years in the desert; and only thus could he guide the Hebrew people to freedom through it. Abraham had to leave everyone he knew (his land and family) to fulfill his patriarchal purpose. Jesus went forty days without eating or drinking in the desert before being invested with power, and he had to drink the cup of the Cross to later be resurrected. God doesn't randomly throw darts to decide His children's future. Every challenge we face has a reason and a purpose. When God pulls you out of your comfort zone, don't complain about the place He took you from. Pay attention to where He is taking you.

> *"When Jesus heard that, He said, 'This sickness is not unto death, but for the glory of God, that the Son of God may be glorified through it.'"*
>
> John 11:4

Prayer: Thank You Lord because every present challenge is a blessing from You that is ready to be given. Help me understand that You always care for me and guide me, and that the apparent threats and obstacles are only a way of strengthening me to give me a better future, to me and my loved ones. Thank You Father. Please increase my faith and courage.

Day 63: God wants to bless me today

"And Jabez called on the God of Israel, saying, 'Oh, that You would bless me indeed, and enlarge my territory, that Your hand would be with me, and that You would keep me from evil, that I may not cause pain!' So God granted him what he requested."

1 Chronicles 4:10

While I was reading this prayer of Jabez, I must confess that I subconsciously expected that at the end, he would promise to do something like, "I will give you my offerings or I will follow You and serve You forever Lord, etc." My mind expected the appropriate sacrifice to obtain such Grace but that isn't what God is like. I had to reread it several times to understand that Jabez was simply invoking his God, manifesting his desire, imagining how good his life and his family's would be if the Lord would give him those four things he meditated on: blessing, expanding his territory, that His hand would be with him and that he would be freed from evil so that no one would suffer harm. Jabez was not offering anything in exchange, just telling his Creator how marvelous it would be to have all that from Him, and God granted it! He granted everything, without any sacrifice in exchange, without penitence, without pain…

Jabez was "more honorable than his brothers" (verse 9), and I think that this was due to his deep spiritual (not religious) understanding. This man didn't focus on himself, on trying to become worthy of receiving something, or maintaining morals without reproach. Neither did he promise to serve in the Church every Sunday (which isn't a bad thing, of course), and it didn't occur to him that he should suffer any type of sacrifice, penitence or torment. He prayed so because he knew the Father and understood God's immense generosity toward His children. What he asked for was what God already wanted to give him. You and I, who are also under His covenant, should learn to ask Him in the same way for all what He already wants to give us. Reading what Jabez craved we could conclude that he was a man of faith: he wanted it all, no less, and he confidently asked the only One who could give it to him. Only a person who keeps communion with God can have the confidence to draw close to Him and ask Him for what his heart desires, like my kids do with me when we pass a store where they find something really attractive. God is a God of reward, but also of favor, and He can grant you the desires of your heart, if they please Him. The question then is: how similar are your heart's desires to His?

> *"Delight yourself also in the Lord, and He shall give you the desires of your heart."*
>
> Psalm 37:4

Prayer: Thank You Father, because you enjoy blessing me and only deny me what I am not yet prepared for. You train me for that, you challenge me and stretch me to give me more. Thank You because my success and plenty do not depend on my virtues but on Your infinite Grace. Bless me, enlarge my territory, let Your hand be always with me and keep me from evil so I don't harm myself or my loved ones. Amen!

Day 64: Today I am reconciled to God and men

"That very day Pilate and Herod became friends with each other, for previously they had been at enmity with each other."

Luke 23:12

Pilate was afraid to condemn Jesus. He knew that there was something wrong about it and tried to transfer the responsibility of making the decision to Herod who, luckily for the former, was in Jerusalem at that moment. The latter, for his part, was excited when he found out he would see Jesus because he hoped the Lord would perform a miracle to entertain him. This king had no fear of God and thought he was over all authority, including the Heavenly authority. But when Jesus didn't respond to any of his many questions or pay attention to his childish requests, the Pharisees and scribes (who went to the palace just to congregate there against the Master) accused Him vehemently while Herod, annoyed because he didn't get the fun he wanted and thought he deserved, together with his soldiers, belittled and mocked Him, and dressed Him in splendid clothes (verses 10-11) to make fun of Him and hit Him. For Jesus, this was just the beginning of His torments…

The Jewish people were waiting for a Messiah who would free them from the hand of their enemy and conqueror: the Romans. However, in their hate against the Lord, they submitted to them even further. This conspiring between staunch enemies, conqueror and conquered, the political power and the religious all only for the purpose of eliminating

Jesus, is one of the greatest proofs of His existence, meaning, and greatness. An army of unholy men, full of evil, found themselves aligned under a single objective, but how is it possible to unite people like that, who were so untrustworthy and with opposing interests? How did they so quickly come to the agreement that the Messiah should die? Because they were under the power of darkness... But Jesus stayed firm, focused, not opening His mouth, and His love is so great that even the arrogant and high-handed rivals (Pilate and Herod) were reconciled through their rejection of Jesus. Truly, the love and power of God have no imaginable limit. He made all things perfect, and the All-Powerful, the High and Lifted Up is more humble than a dry leaf or the ashes in a chimney. Therefore, if we follow His example, we reconcile ourselves primarily to Him and then we ask Him to help us reconcile to our loved ones, friends, and of course, our enemies.

> *"But if you do not forgive men their trespasses, neither will your Father forgive your trespasses."*
>
> Matthew 6:15

Prayer: Holy Spirit, help me to forgive those who have hurt me. Free me from souvenirs of the past, of all lack of forgiveness in my soul, of all resentment that embitters me. Restore my soul, my thoughts. Clean me with Your love. I know that if I don't forgive, You cannot forgive me because we have all sinned. Guide me Lord. Soften my pride.

Day 65: Today I receive health in my body and soul

"And when the Pharisees saw it, they said to His disciples, 'Why does your Teacher eat with tax collectors and sinners?' When Jesus heard that, He said to them, 'Those who are well have no need of a physician, but those who are sick.'"

Matthew 9:11-12

When Adam and Eve ate (considered, chewed, digested) the fruit of the tree of knowledge of good and evil, the latter (they already knew the good) entered into their minds and hearts for the first time. Like a little pipe of black water that empties into the clean river, sin entered into the soul of man and separation with God, duality, followed: good and evil, life and death, blessing and curse. God had warned them that if they ate this fruit they would surely die (Genesis 2:17), but He wasn't saying that they would immediately pass away physically (in fact, both lived many years after their expulsion from the Garden of Eden), but that they would lose their spiritual communion with Him. And so it was. Separation was born. In that moment, although it was invisible to Adam and Eve's eyes, a seed of death from Satan was planted in their souls... And its fruit passes from generation to generation, until a child is raised up to invoke the name of Jesus, and breaks the curse (Galatians 3:13).

Once more, the Jews sought arguments to criticize and attack Jesus, and to do that they tried to judge His behavior (he ate with corrupt fishermen), but He, on the other hand, didn't defend Himself. Instead He responded in terms of health. Jesus knows that the origin of illness is sin. That's why He has to first heal our soul—take out the resentment, the shame, the greed and envy, and cure with infinite paternal love, every one of the bindings that torment and oppress us, so that we can be completely free. That's why Peter says that love "will cover a multitude of sins" (1 Peter 4:8). Illness is not God's punishment for sin. What happens is that seed of separation and death passes from generation to generation, and in the same way that only Jesus can clean you of your sins, only He can completely free you; pull out, expel, and eradicate all roots of illness (spiritual, mental, and physical). He is the excellent Healer. All the sick were healed and freed in His Presence, without exception, and He is the same today and forever. Let Him fill you with Himself; receive a transfusion of His precious blood, poured out on Calvary for you. Your body's health begins in your soul:

> *"And He said to her, 'Daughter, your faith has made you* [her soul] *well. Go in peace, and be healed of your affliction* [her body]. *"*
>
> Mark 5:34

Prayer: Dear Jesus, free me from all religiosity and give me a sincere heart before You. Help me not to judge so I won't be judged. Save me and free me from all afflictions. In the name of Jesus, amen!

Day 66: Today I am guided by Your Spirit

"For as many as are led by the Spirit of God, these are sons of God."

Romans 8:14

In the natural world you can ignore and even detest your father and keep calling yourself his son or daughter, but it isn't so in the spiritual world. In fact, the decision of whether or not we are called God's children doesn't rest on us but on Him. After all, it is the father who recognizes the child and not the reverse; and a child doesn't adopt the father, but the opposite. It is a catastrophe that humanity confuses having been created by God with the privilege of being His children, just as it confuses respecting a moral code (religion) with having a relationship with God's Spirit. The two are very different…

What is it that you enjoy most about your children, the fun times with them, or their perfect behavior because they respect all your commands (sometimes out of fear, of course)? Your morals are never going to make you worthy of God, nor are they going to get you to Heaven. That is why Solomon wrote, "Every way of a man is right in his own eyes, but the Lord weighs the hearts" (Proverbs 21:2). What makes you God's child is not your own justice or sharing with those who you consider less spiritual, but rather being "led by the Spirit of God," because only "these are the sons of God." I constantly hear phrases like "I have my own god," or "I relate to Him in my own way," but the truth is that we can only relate to God in His way, not ours. He is Lord, not us! Only our ignorance together with our arrogance, dare to claim that we define and sustain that relationship. Is a baby, perhaps, the one who decides how to be cared for? Is a child, perhaps, the one who chooses how to be disciplined? Many of us play the role of a rebellious teen who dreams about dominating, being the one who decides, the one who controls, but we are just like the mischievous child who cries in the store to pressure mama to buy a toy… Fortunately, God cannot be manipulated. In John 15:4, Jesus says, "You are My friends if you do whatever I command you." In this context "do whatever I command you" means to treasure His teachings, appreciate His counsel, value His Grace. According to the Bible, only the one who treasures the counsel of His Father is worthy of being called His son, and you can't treasure His Word if you don't spend time at His feet, listening to it or reading it. Don't wait any longer; seek Him from your heart:

> *"But 'he who glories, let him glory in the Lord;' for not he who commends himself is approved, but whom the Lord commends."*
>
> 2 Corinthians 4:18

Prayer: Holy Spirit, guide me. I have no greater desire than to be guided by Your Spirit; I have no greater desire than to be called Your child. Help me listen to Your voice, to understand Your will and not hesitate to obey You diligently, always. Thank you for being such a good Father.

Day 67: Today I give glory only to God

"How can you believe, who receive honor from one another, and do not seek the honor that comes from the only God?"

John 5:44

Do you know why some people don't believe in Jesus? Because they receive (and give) glory from each other. Have you noticed how many leaders, artists and sports stars are worshipped as idols (a much higher level of exaltation than what we could call "admiring")? Controversial characters in the media are exalted and blindly followed for their riches and eccentricities despite how little respectability is in their conduct, and frequently, in their disastrous lives. Politicians think they own the nations they lead; artists ready to do anything to stay "in the limelight;" sports stars enter the court with the arrogance of a king, entering a city they just conquered. In my country, Venezuela, some admirers of the deceased president Chavez call him "the supreme and eternal commander," but there is only One who is Eternal and Supreme ("far above…every name that has been named" Ephesians 1:21), and if we believed in Him more, we would give less glory to other people. The problem is not that we honor men. There is nothing wrong with a healthy admiration for those who inspire us. The problem, according to what Jesus explains here, is that when people receive glory from each other, we minimize the Lord, and that's why we don't believe in Him. Can you understand, beyond pure intellect that, for example, the universe is trillions of times larger than our solar system? Can you really picture it? If like me, it is impossible for you to envision it, maybe it's because the sun, proportionally small, looks larger and brighter from the earth due to the simple fact that it is closer to us. In the same way, if you focus on man, you can't imagine the magnificence of the Creator. I believe that one aspect of Jesus's character that allowed him to maintain a life free of sin and to persevere through all temptation, literally unto death (having the absolute power to free Himself in His hands, Matthew 26:53), is because He only sought glory for His Abba. That is why He said, "I do not receive honor from men" (John 5:41). Admire, imitate the good, let yourself be inspired by great personalities and inspire others around you. But use extreme caution with flatterers, because it's easy to fall in the trap of their mouths, forgetting who the Lord and King is. Never take glory that doesn't belong to you, and don't give it to others:

> *"But he who glories, let him glory in the Lord; for not he who commends himself is approved, but whom the Lord commends."*
>
> 1 Corinthians 10:17-18

Prayer: Father bless me, but don't let me ever glory in myself. Only in You Lord, only in You. Let me walk every day of my life seeking Your glory, not mine Lord. I want you to always be my first option, my priority, the essential and the first fruits of my life, time and money to always be for You. Thank you Jesus.

Day 68: Today I see the living God

"Then, as they were afraid and bowed their faces to the earth, they said to them 'Why do you seek the living among the dead?'"

Luke 24:5

Mary Magdalene and other women had gone very early to the sepulcher with aromatic spices to honor and anoint the body of the Lord, but the stone had been removed. While they were perplexed by what had happened, two "men...in shining garments" asked them the question that I love most in the whole Bible. A question that destroys all idolatry, all religions and external rituals with their human traditions, and all adoration of relics and images with nine words: "Why do you seek the living among the dead?"

Jesus Christ died in the most painful death possible, crucified; but He also resurrected after being among the dead. He was made poor, but only so that through His poverty you and I would be enriched (2 Corinthians 8:9). He was cursed, but only so that we would be blessed once His sacrifice was complete (Galatians 3:13). He was wounded and crushed for our sins, but only thus could He erase our rebellions and mistakes (Isaiah 53:5). His immaculate body was wounded, but there, we all, through His pain, were cured (Isaiah 53:5). They abused His head with a crown of thorns (Matthew 27:29) to plant discord in His mind, but they couldn't do it, and on top of that He gave us the mind of Christ (1 Corinthians 2:16). The highest political power and the highest religious power were united, for the first time in history and under the guidance of evil, to destroy Him but they couldn't do it. Enemies for generations now worked together against Him, but Christ won! He didn't found a religion or a political party. Jesus is not a socialist, capitalist, or communist. He is not an activist or a feminist. He is the King of kings and Lord of lords, the Alpha and Omega, the Beginning and the End, the Creator of the Heavens and the Earth, the Redeemer, the Savior of the world, the Liberator, the Prince of Peace. He doesn't dwell in crucifixes or buildings but rather in His children. If you believe Him, He moves into you and makes His temple there. Don't seek Him among the dead because He is alive. You don't look for water in cemeteries, or hope in dry bones. He died, but He rose. Find His immense love on the cross, but look for His hope in the open tomb, because He is the same "yesterday, and today, and forever." (Hebrews 13:8)

> *"And they said among themselves, 'Who will roll away the stone from the door of the tomb for us?' But when they looked up, they saw that the stone had been rolled away—for it was very large."*
>
> Mark 16:3-4

Prayer: Today I let go of all human attempts to represent Your Glory through religion. Today I renounce all idolatry and center myself on You, who are Life. I seek You within me and around me, not in dead objects or in the traditions of man. Thank You Jehovah.

Day 69: Today I give God all the glory

"The king shall have joy in Your strength, O Lord; and in Your salvation how greatly shall he rejoice!"

Psalm 21:1

David was a very powerful king—a great leader, famous and rich who, despite this, knew where his power and salvation came from: God. David didn't take glory from outside; rather, He honored the One who gave it to him. Can you imagine a new president of your country who, at the moment of assuming his position, recognizes in front of the media and the whole nation, that his power comes only from God, and that along with his happiness about his success, he rejoices in God for His salvation? Or the CEO of the company where you work, calling out to God for His favor when he takes the job or begins a new contract? That is exactly the humility and level-headedness that we all need... Not only a president or a boss--all of us! That's why God tells us, once we reach the good that He has promised us, not to turn to Him and say, "My power and the might of my hand have gained me this wealth" (Deuteronomy 8:17).

And you, do you rejoice when you see God's power in your life, or do you forget Him the instant that the problem is resolved or the challenge has been overcome? Many of us cry out to God in need, but few of us do it when we smile with success; many ask for help in battle, but few celebrate victory with Him. The moment we overcome our difficulty, our mind is distracted, and in the midst of complacency, our old ego slips through, silently, and takes over our glory. But throughout the Bible, we see that the most successful characters seek and honor God in the good and bad, sick or healthy, in abundance or scarcity. God isn't worthy when He grants you something; rather, He is always worthy because He is Lord of the universe. He isn't worthy because He blessed you; He created you and bought you before you were born, giving His own Son up for you, to give you life. His majesty doesn't depend on whether or not things are going well for you. Would the president of your country stopped being president when you got sick, were discouraged or faced economic problems? Of course he will not. What He deserves is independent from you and how your issues are going. That is why David declared, "I will bless the Lord at all times; His praise shall continually be in my mouth" (Psalm 34:1). What if we focused a little less on our problems and a little more on His greatness? Less on what we need and more on what we already have? Let's be thankful, happy to have His power in our lives, and rejoice for His salvation.

"... for without Me you can do nothing." John 15:5b

Prayer: Together with David, I declare that there is no good for me apart from You, Lord. I recognize that You are the only source of all good in my life, in my family, on earth and in the universe. That all blessing and spiritual, intellectual, emotional, physical, social and material gifts are provided by Your generosity and Your benevolence. Thank You for creating such a marvelous place like the planet where You put us, Lord.

Day 70: Today I give the control to the One who is in control

"Are not five sparrows sold for two copper coins? And not one of them is forgotten before God. But the very hairs of your head are all numbered. Do not fear therefore; you are of more value than many sparrows."

Luke 12:6-7

What it is that keeps you up at night? Is there something causing anxiety because you can't find the solution, the path, the answer? I remember a flight where in the middle of unpleasant turbulence that wouldn't let me relax, a baby slept soundly, hugged in his mother's lap. I think that little one knew that even the few hairs of his head were counted, and that He, before his Father, is worth more than many sparrows. So now, why can't we realize how valuable we are? What is it that keeps us apart from the truth and blocks our ability to believe God's Word? Why can't we live in peace, seeing ourselves how He sees us and knowing that He indeed cares for us and loves us?

We are genetically programmed to survive, and for that reason, we feel an intense need for control. We want to feel safe, and frequently, pursuing this security, we risk something much greater: our soul. On one hand, we know that something greater exists, that there is something "out there," but on the other, we put more trust in what we can see and feel, and so we invent an abstract god, not very real, a godwho sometimes hears and other times doesn't, who helps some but not others. But that is absurd and unbiblical, and only a crazy person would pray to a god they don't believe in. God is One (Deuteronomy 6:4) and doesn't show partiality to people (Deuteronomy 10:17, Acts 10:34). We have to reprogram ourselves until we understand the person of God, the Holy Spirit. He can't guide you if you don't seek His guidance; He can't instruct you if you don't believe Him; He can't speak to someone who doesn't have time to listen or a humble heart that wants to learn. How would you counsel a son who always ignored you, who didn't listen, who didn't value your opinion at all, and who, instead of having a thankful heart, only held rebellion toward you? I tell you with certainty, God has not forgotten you, but maybe you have forgotten Him. Reconcile with Him, right now; do not wait any more! Jesus Christ rebuilt the bridge so you would have direct access to Him and live in peace, you and your loved ones, but you need to believe Him:

> *"But without faith it is impossible to please Him, for he who comes to God must believe that He is, and that He is a rewarder of those who diligently seek Him."*
>
> Hebrews 11:6

Prayer: Lord, forgive my rebellions and arrogance. I want to reconcile with You and release the excessive control that I try to impose on my life. I am not god. You are Lord God. Forgive my boasting, Lord. Transform me. Help me to spend more time with You. Amen!

Day 71: Today I only adore the true God

"The idols of the nations are silver and gold, the work of men's hands. They have mouths, but they do not speak; eyes they have, but they do not see; they have ears, but they do not hear, nor is there any breath in their mouths. Those who make them are like them; so is everyone who trusts in them."

Psalm 135:15-18

At the first opportunity, when Moses left the people alone, they built a golden heifer and began to worship it (Deuteronomy 9:16). Isn't that incredible? They had seen God's wrath fall as plagues over Egypt, the column of fire every night and the cloud covering them by day; they had eaten the manna that fell from the sky, drunk the water from a spring and delighted in quail when they asked for meat. How could they have forgotten it all so quickly and worshipped an object? How could they seek the One, who had opened the sea before their own eyes, in a statue? In spite of their freedom, they were still slaves. They wanted to worship God, but they didn't know Him. Only by knowing the truth will we be free (John 8:31-32), while we perish because we lack knowledge (Hosea 4:6).

Like the bat who ignores daylight from inside the cave, we obviate the Spiritual, blinded by the natural. We believe in what we can see and feel, committing a grave error because the spiritual world is more real than the visible one (2 Corinthians 4:18). That's why Jesus said, "Blessed are those who have not seen and yet have believed" (John 20:29). We should learn to worship the One who we cannot see, with absolute certainty;

to submit to Him as if we were "seeing Him who is invisible" (Hebrews 11:27), and use the lenses of His Word to interpret everything. Paul says that faith is "the evidence of things not seen" (Hebrews 11:1b), because although we can't measure or embrace it, it is real. All representations of God limit our perception of Him. Those images "have mouths, but do not speak," while God does; they don't have "breath in their mouths," but God put life in yours. Would you fall in love with a mannequin? No, because you know that it doesn't contain a human spirit. So then, how could it contain God's? If we trust in an image, we make ourselves like it, because we offend God instead of exalting him. We "package" Him. Far from increasing your faith, it limits it. That's why our Creator, who wants to open us up, expand us, lift us up, also orders us:

> *"You shall have no other gods before Me. You shall not make for yourself a carved image--any likeness of anything that is in heaven above, or that is in the earth beneath, or that is in the water under the earth; "you shall not bow down to them nor serve them. For I, the Lord your God, am a jealous God…"*
>
> Exodus 20:3-5

Prayer: Today I reject all forms of idolatry, because I know that it offends You and hurts You Lord, because when I limit You in my mind, I lose many of Your blessings. Today I declare myself free, in Jesus's Name, of all links to religious objects, to witchcraft and idolatry. Amen.

Day 72: *Today I let the Lord work in me*

"Whoever has been born of God does not sin, for His seed remains in him; and he cannot sin, because he has been born of God."

1 John 3:9

To sin means to err, and it happens when we make decisions that oppose God's will. We all sin (Romans 3:23) but it is one thing to make a mistake and another very different, to practice sinning. When you try to be better according to your own morals and you try to get rid of bad habits and customs, you do something very good and respectable; but frequently, it's like pruning a tree. Sooner or later the branch grows back, and with the same fruit. But when you receive Christ as your only and all sufficient Savior, when you invite Him to dwell in you, He makes you a new creation instead (2 Corinthians 5:17); you are born again, but "*of God.*" Now the very root is transformed, and as such, so are the tree, the branches, the leaves, flowers, and fruit. When you see the new fruit you don't remember how the plant was before, because it's different now. The same happens with you. You can make mistakes, of course, but you can't practice sin anymore.

I don't know what practice or bad habit you want to be freed from today. I don't know what kind of mistake you want to get away from so your life and the lives of those you love can move forward with real satisfaction. I don't know what you want to be free of. Maybe a tendency to eat too much, a violent personality or a sexual practice that degrades you; or it could be that habit of underestimating and assaulting others and yourself. Maybe it's your pride that is out of control, or you have a secret addiction that doesn't let you sleep in peace. Whatever it is: don't keep fighting it with your own strength. Sin, when it is interlaced into your soul, cannot be defeated with discipline or perseverance, but only with the Blood of Christ. Your character is not going to be really transformed from constantly paying attention to it; rather, it will be transformed by the Presence of the Holy Spirit. It's not about you or me but about Him, in us. It's not about what He will do for you but about what He already did. Don't try to change the surface; let Him transform your inside. It's not makeup; it's being born again. It's not about doing something either, but that you let Him work in you. Don't toil, trying to get the bad out of you. Instead, let He who is good, enter in; don't fight darkness, just turn on His light. Let Him fill you with His love, His holiness, His power. If you sincerely invite Him to be Lord of your life, to exercise loving dominion over your soul, if you offer Him a comfortable seat in your mind and desire to sit at His table, of course you can make mistakes, but you cannot sin.

"We are of God. He who knows God hears us; he who is not of God does not hear us. By this we know the spirit of truth and the spirit of error."

1 John 4:6

Prayer: Today I let You work in me, Lord. Today I recognize You as my only and all sufficient Lord and Savior, and I let you direct my life. Today I confess that I cannot do it myself because, apart from You, I can do nothing. Today I don't fight evil, but I let the Good enter. Today I no longer fight darkness; instead I let You, the Light, come in. Thank You Lord, because you free and restore me.

Day 73: Today I begin my new life in Christ

"...that you put off, concerning your former conduct, the old man which grows corrupt according to the deceitful lusts ..."

Ephesians 4:22

No one puts on a new suit over an old, dirty one. Instead, they take the former off completely, take a bath, and clean up well to put on the new one. No one occupies a new house without sweeping and cleaning every corner first. Only after cleaning you will bring your family in, furniture, and personal objects. What's more, when we invite someone whom we admire a lot or who is very important, into our home, we clean and organize every area. We pull out the best dishes and make sure that everything is impeccable and presentable. However, many of us, even though we say that God is the most important thing in our lives, sincerely invite the Holy Spirit to dwell in us while we keep thick cobwebs in the corners of our mind and dark stains inside our heart. So we ask Him for a new suit, white and clean while we want to keep wearing the same old underwear, worn and smelly, like someone who sweeps the dirt under the rug.

But Paul tells us here that this belongs to the past, to our old, former way of living, and that we should take off that old suit, expel that egocentric and arrogant "me" that is so concerned about what others do or how they dress; who seeks satisfaction in acquiring what it doesn't need, and whose priority is receiving more and giving less, because it is impure (it has vice, false need) because of deceptive desires (it thinks it needs what it doesn't need). Many live their lives comparing themselves to others, wanting what others have, trying to do what others do and to achieve what others achieve. It seems their objectives in life are completely connected to others, and only by becoming equal to or greater than others can they feel successful. But this will always be wrong, because wherever you are and go there will always be someone ahead of you, and someone behind you. Maybe today would be a good day to look over your priorities and discover the One who you really do need. Maybe today you can be concerned a little more about your spouse, recognize your children, or motivate others. Be encouraged; get rid of that old you, and start admiring and pleasing God and those around you. Let His living water refresh your soul. Take off the old you right now and give way to the new, better you that you can be, that will only bloom when you give space to Him.

"Therefore, if anyone is in Christ, he is a new creation; old things have passed away; behold, all things have become new."
2 Corinthians 5:17

Prayer: Lord Jesus, thank You for recreating me, for making me a new creation in You. My dirty, smelly clothes were replaced by new ones, white and clean, according to Your holiness and power. Father, enter into me so this cleanness will remain in my entire being forever.

Day 74: You are always good

"So Jesus said to him, 'Why do you call Me good? No one is good but One, that is, God.'"

Mark 10:18

I recently found out about a person who, because his little girl had appendicitis, made a deal with God, saying, "Lord, if You heal my daughter, I will stop drinking that coffee I like so much for forty days." I would love to ask him what he demanded of his child to get him to take her to the hospital. I'm sure he would answer, "Nothing, of course. I did it because I love her," and I would ask, "And God doesn't?" For centuries, religion has taught us that God is moved by pain and pity, that sins are erased with penitence and not with Christ's blood, that God's discipline exceeds His Grace. That is why "penitence" is so frequent, because we don't understand His love. If it were so, what kind of Father would the Lord be? Would you give an illness to one of your children to correct them or "deal with" them? Someone once told me, "When God wants me to rest, He gives me some flu and puts me in bed for two days." It's obvious that this person doesn't understand God's love. He is always, only, good.

Do you like your children to ask you for what they want while crying? I suppose not. I personally detest manipulation like that, so neither pity nor drama moves me to pay attention to them. But when we have our long walks, talking one on one with them, it's different. The more we share, the more we know each other, and by opening our hearts, we love each other even more. There I counsel them and bless them. In the same way, what He wants is your attention; your ears attentive to His love and His counsel, to be able to bless you, free you, and restore you. He desires to relate to you more. He has never done you any harm or damage. He has always given you much more than what pleases you or what you can even perceive. He has always been the source of so many opportunities that you have dismissed, and even today, He keeps knocking at the door of your heart without you opening it. God isn't unjust or mean, and attributing characteristics to Him that He doesn't have is blasphemy, a grave sin that we should repent of. God corrects; He doesn't hurt. He disciplines; He doesn't attack. He protects; He doesn't destroy. He frees; He doesn't enslave. He is Life, not death. He heals; He doesn't make you sick. He forgives; He doesn't condemn. He is Blessing, not curse. He prospers you; He doesn't impoverish you. He is good, not bad. Be careful not to attribute Him what He is not, becoming His judge. Know Him more and you will discover that He is always only and exclusively good…

> *"Every good gift and every perfect gift is from above, and comes down from the Father of lights, with whom there is no variation or shadow of turning."*
>
> James 1:17

Prayer: Thank You Father, because you are not moved by pain or pity. You cannot be manipulated. You confide in us and challenge us to give us more and so we can live better. Today I get rid of all thoughts of penitence and suffering. Today I understand that you are a good Father. Only the devil is an oppressor but You freed us from him, forever. Thank You Jesus Christ.

Day 75: Today I choose God, for me and my loved ones

"I call heaven and earth as witnesses today against you, that I have set before you life and death, blessing and cursing; therefore choose life, that both you and your descendants may live;"

Deuteronomy 30:19

In Bible times, the testimony of two or more witnesses was required to accuse someone (See Matthew 18:16, 2 Corinthians 13:11), which is why God, here, in His absolute faithfulness to His own Word, presents us with a pair of uncommon witnesses: heaven and earth. He uses them to confront us with an irrefutable truth. No matter how confusing the circumstances or how difficult the challenges seem, human beings will always have two options, two possibilities to choose from: God, or no God. In every circumstance He places before us "life and death, blessing and curse," good and bad, straight and twisted, constructive and destructive, worthy and unworthy, high and low, truth and lie... We are the ones who chose, not Him, and whether we want it or not, whether it seems fair or not, each of these decisions brings a specific consequence with it. Many people think that they can choose evil and live well, curse and be blessed, sow pain in others and harvest happiness in themselves, build happiness on someone else's disgrace and prosper from someone else's scarcity, but it isn't possible. Paul says that "God is not mocked; for whatever a man sows, that he will also reap" (Galatians 6:7), and Jesus says, "Do men gather grapes from thorn bushes or figs from thistles?" (Matthew 7:16) Only if you choose life will you live— "you and your descendants." If you choose evil, accept it when it knocks at your door and don't blame God for the result of your decisions.

God engraved His morals in our conscience and the conviction of His existence, saying, "I will put My law in their minds, and write it on their hearts; and I will be their God, and they shall be My people" (Jeremiah 31:33); but we have become rebels, believing we are self-sufficient, making decisions according to our "own understanding" (Proverbs 3:5). Today, God invites us to choose Him, to do His will, to seek His guidance. In the famous film "Mrs. Doubtfire," Robin Williams, disguised as a nanny, breathlessly watches her youngest daughter jumps into the arms of the beau who seems to not only court his ex-wife, but also his children. How exasperating! I wouldn't be able to stand my children calling another man Papa... However, we repeatedly do that with God. We say we are His children, but at the smallest challenge, we jump into the arms of other gods: pleasure, status, comfort zone, power, money, acceptance, and even "what will they say." But it is written:

"You shall have no other gods before Me."

Exodus 20:3

Prayer: Today I renounce idolatry and I focus only on You, Lord. Today, I understand how it hurts You when we separate from You and give glory to others, to our own detriment. Today I choose the life and blessing that only come from Christ so that my family, all my descendants and I can live in fullness.

Lord Jesus, I beg you to enter into my soul now.
I believe in my heart that you carried all my sins on the Cross.

I confess with my mouth that You are the Son of God, and that
God lifted You up from among the dead
Come, I beg you. I want you to be the Lord of my life

I renounce all deals with the enemy, made by me,
my parents, my grandparents, and all my ancestors to the fourth
generation, together with my uncles and aunts, and all my cousins.

I renounce and repent of all idolatry, of all
participation in the occult and every corrupt word
that I have spoken at any moment of my life.

Today, by Your Grace, I receive the only covenant, with Your blood
on the Cross of Calvary, and according to what is written: at that
moment I pass from the power of darkness to the Light of Christ

Today I receive salvation through Your sacrifice, health
through Your wounds, prosperity because You carried my
poverty and blessing because You were cursed for me

Thank You because Your Word says that You will never
cast out the one who comes to you… Amen!